BLACK FATIGUE

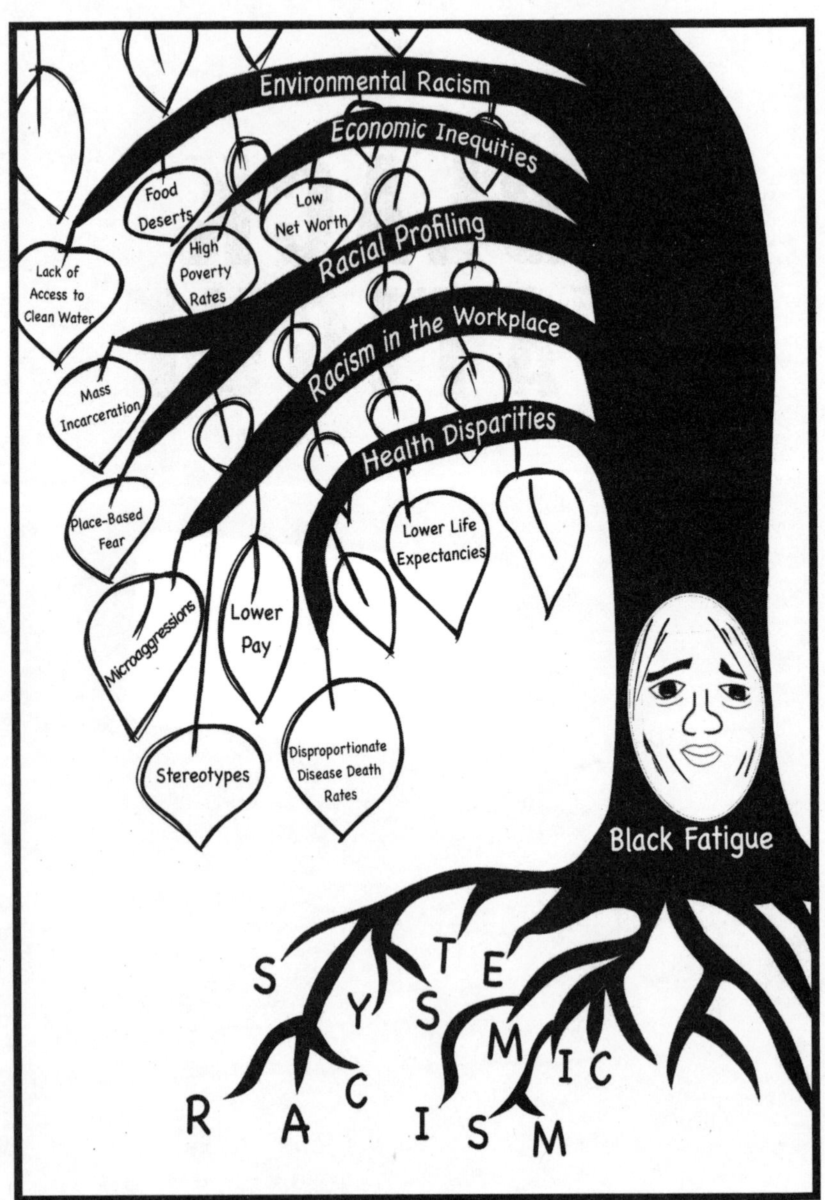

Environmental Racism
Economic Inequities
Food Deserts
Low Net Worth
High Poverty Rates
Lack of Access to Clean Water
Racial Profiling
Racism in the Workplace
Mass Incarceration
Health Disparities
Place-Based Fear
Lower Life Expectancies
Microaggressions
Lower Pay
Stereotypes
Disproportionate Disease Death Rates
Black Fatigue
SYSTEMIC RACISM

BLACK FATIGUE

How Racism Erodes the Mind, Body, and Spirit

MARY-FRANCES WINTERS

Berrett–Koehler Publishers, Inc.

Berrett-Koehler Publishers, Inc.
1333 Broadway, Suite 1000
Oakland, CA 94612-1921
Tel: (510) 817-2277
Fax: (510) 817-2278
www.bkconnection.com

ORDERING INFORMATION

Quantity sales. Special discounts are available on quantity purchases by corporations, associations, and others. For details, contact the "Special Sales Department" at the Berrett-Koehler address above.

Individual sales. Berrett-Koehler publications are available through most bookstores. They can also be ordered directly from Berrett-Koehler: Tel: (800) 929-2929; Fax: (802) 864-7626; www.bkconnection.com.

Orders for college textbook / course adoption use. Please contact Berrett-Koehler: Tel: (800) 929-2929; Fax: (802) 864-7626.

Distributed to the U.S. trade and internationally by Penguin Random House Publisher Services.

Printed in Canada

Berrett-Koehler books are printed on long-lasting acid-free paper. When it is available, we choose paper that has been manufactured by environmentally responsible processes. These may include using trees grown in sustainable forests, incorporating recycled paper, minimizing chlorine in bleaching, or recycling the energy produced at the paper mill.

Library of Congress Control Number: 2020941572

First Edition
30 29 28 27 26 25 24 23 22 21 20 10 9 8 7 6 5 4 3 2 1

Book production by Westchester Publishing Services
Frontispiece and chapter opener art © The Winters Group, Inc. Art by Krystle Nicholas
Cover design by Mike Nicholls
MARTIN typeface by Vocal Type Co.
Los Feliz typeface by Emigre Fonts

To the generations of freedom fighters, civil rights leaders,
and social justice advocates who preceded me
in the ongoing quest for liberation.

And especially to those who lost their lives in the struggle.
Without their sacrifice, my voice would not be possible.

CONTENTS

PREFACE

Note on capitalization: I capitalize "Black" and lowercase "white" when referring to these two identity groups to follow Brookings' recent decision, after months of research, to change its style guide in this way. Brookings' rationale is as follows: "It is an act in recognition of racial respect for those who have been generations in the 'lower case.'"[1]

When I conceived the idea for *Black Fatigue* in the fall of 2019, Black colleagues and friends urged me to write it as soon as possible. They said we need to chronicle the fear, frustration, anguish, and, yes, rage that is a regular part of many Black people's daily lives and how it affects the mind, body, and spirit. "Living while Black" is a term coined to embrace the myriad unjust and inequitable experiences that are relentless and too often lead to violence against Black people.

This was before the COVID-19 outbreak in January 2020 and the global, organized, and powerful rebellions against systemic racism that started in May 2020. These events changed the world as we know it forever and served to put a spotlight on Black fatigue.

Hundreds of thousands of people all over the world died from the highly contagious virus, for which there was no vaccine at the time. Black and Brown people were disproportionately affected, dying at rates two to four times the rate of white people. Black people were also more likely to lose their jobs during the pandemic or have essential jobs that meant greater exposure to the disease. Shelter-in-place orders were enacted, and food and other essentials were scarce. Makeshift hospitals were set up to accommodate the surge in cases, and miles-long lines of cars waiting for food rations were common. People all over the world were enduring unimaginable stress and pain. Black people were even more severely affected.

And then, over the course of 30 days in the spring of 2020, the public learned of the tragic deaths of Ahmaud Arbery, Breonna Taylor, and George Floyd. They were unarmed Black people killed at the hands of law enforcement. There were others who did not get the same media attention, such as Tony McDade, a Black transgender man who was killed by the police in Florida, though the reports indicate that the circumstances around his death are "murky." Nina Pop, a Black transgender woman, was stabbed to death in Missouri in a possible hate crime. Two Black men were found hanging from trees in neighboring communities in California under suspicious circumstances.

George Floyd's murder was the tipping point. Many sat in disbelief and horror as they watched the video footage, taken by a 17-year-old girl, of Minneapolis police officer Derek Chauvin, with his hands in his pockets, blatantly and cavalierly pressing his knee against Floyd's neck for 8 minutes and 46 seconds. Floyd pleaded for his life. He said 15 times, "I can't breathe, officer." He was pronounced dead at the scene, and it would be days before any charges were brought against Chauvin and weeks before charges were brought against the other three officers involved. In the case of Ahmaud Arbery, he was gunned down in Georgia as he was jogging in his neighborhood; the public did not hear of it for almost two months, and it took another month for the perpetrators (self-proclaimed law enforcers) to be arrested. Breonna Taylor was in her apartment in Louisville, Kentucky, when police, executing a no-knock search warrant for drugs in the middle of the night, shot her at least eight times. They had entered the wrong house.

These tragic incidents in a short time span in 2020 amplified, in gory detail, the centuries-old, willful disregard for Black lives. We were reminded of the period in our history when Black men were lynched, put on public display as a means of terrorizing and controlling. These recent deaths are examples of modern-day lynching. And there are so many more examples throughout history of Black people being targeted and killed. One of the most famous atrocities is that of Emmett Till, the 14-year-old who was lynched in Mississippi in 1955 for allegedly whistling at a white woman.[2] There are a number of high-profile cases in recent history, such as those of Trayvon Martin (2012), Michael Brown (2014), Tamir Rice (2014), Botham Jean (2019), Philando Castile (2016), and Eric Garner (2014). A NewsOne report released in June, shares the stories of 83 Black men and boys that have been killed by police since 2012.[3]

Around the same time as George Floyd's murder, Amy Cooper (a white woman) was walking her dog in Central Park and Christian Cooper (not related, a Black man) was bird-watching. He requested that she keep her dog leashed in accordance with park regulations. She refused to do so, and a verbal dispute ensued, with Ms. Cooper calling 911, ranting that an African American man was threatening her and her dog. Mr. Cooper remained calm throughout the ordeal, urging her to call authorities. Ms. Cooper was fired from her job at a large financial services company.

With the Black community already at a heightened level of stress from dealing with the multiple disparate impacts of COVID-19 on Black people, these all-too-familiar racist incidents were the proverbial straw that broke the camel's back. They sparked monthlong fervent protests by people across the spectrum of diversity who globally denounced police brutality and demanded racial justice. These rebellions, mostly peaceful, signaled a new movement against anti-Black racism that proclaimed, enough is enough. We are exhausted from dealing with racism and violence against Black people. Symbols of racism such as confederate flags and other historical monuments were dismantled forcibly, and in other cases, lawmakers decided to remove them.

When I conceived the idea for *Black Fatigue*, I certainly could not have foretold the imminence of this renewed demand for racial justice. The accumulated pain and trauma from centuries of violence perpetrated against Black people reached the boiling point. It was inevitable because history has taught us that oppressed people will rebel when they just cannot take it anymore.

In response to this outcry to end racism, many organizations seemed to wake up overnight with a frenzied sense of urgency and began to develop new strategies and initiatives. They issued statements of solidarity, scheduled town hall sessions with all employees to proclaim their commitment to ensuring racist-free work environments and pledged millions of dollars to organizations focused on eradicating racism. The Winters Group was retained by several companies to conduct sessions with Black employees to provide a safe space for them to share their feelings and with white employees to summarize the history of racism and provide guidelines for allyship.

Perhaps not surprisingly, many white people claim to not have much understanding of why Black people are fatigued. We conduct a poll during virtual sessions with white employees that asks, How much knowledge do you have about the history of racism in the United States? Only about 10 percent of the mostly white audiences say that they are very knowledgeable. This book will provide a great resource to enhance white people's education.

In the sessions with Black employees, they overwhelmingly reported that they were already exhausted and, because of the events of 2020, they were now downright fatigued. They openly shared stories of the emotional burden of living and working in spaces that diminish their existence. Many were skeptical that the proclamations by their organizations to do a better job of creating safe and welcoming environments for Black employees were more than empty promises.

In 2013, before the 2020 rebellions for racial justice, the Black Lives Matter movement was started by three young women in response to the acquittal of George Zimmerman, who killed 17-year-old Trayvon Martin as he walked home from the store with a bag of Skittles. Now known as the Black Lives Matter Global Network with chapters around the world, its purpose is to intervene when violence is inflicted on Black communities. This new age of activism ignited by millennials (1980–1996) and members of Generation Z (1997–2012) is reminiscent of the civil rights movement of the 1960s. For example, the Black Panther

Party for Self-Defense was born, in part, out of a response to the killing of Matthew Johnson, an unarmed Black 16-year-old, in San Francisco in 1966.

Black Fatigue highlights the history of white supremacist, racist systems that have led to Black intergenerational fatigue. It focuses on the impact of Black fatigue not only on Blacks but also on society. The racist system is not just literally killing Black people; it is tearing the whole nation apart. In every aspect of life, from socioeconomics to education, the workforce, criminal justice, and, very importantly, health outcomes, for the most part the trajectory for Black people is not improving. It is paradoxical that with all the attention over the last 50 years on social justice and diversity and inclusion, we have made little progress in actualizing the vision of an equitable society.

I have been concerned for some time that the modern-day diversity movement, especially in corporate America, obfuscates racial issues that are unique to Black people. So often, I have been cautioned not to focus too much on race in diversity sessions. Of all the popular diversity topics (age, sex, gender identity, disability), white people, by and large, are most uncomfortable talking about race—especially Black people. It may be because of internalized white guilt. My hope is that, as a result of the new racial justice movement, the corporate world will no longer minimize the issues of Black people.

I ask white people to read this book not only to be educated on the history of racism but also to be motivated to become an antiracist, an ally, and a power broker for systemic change.

For Black, Indigenous, and other people of color (BIPOC) who read this book, I hope that it will also be educational and affirming, and that when one of your white colleagues asks you to educate them, you can refer them to this resource, so as not to exacerbate your fatigue.

Our lives have no meaning, no depth without the white gaze. And I have spent my entire writing life trying to make sure that the white gaze was not the dominant one in any of my books.

—Toni Morrison, American novelist, essayist, book editor, and college professor

INTRODUCTION

Black Fatigue Runs Deep

Jumaane D. Williams is a Black man. He is a New York City public advocate. In passionate and tear-filled extemporaneous comments at a press conference regarding the killing of Ahmaud Arbery, Breonna Taylor, and George Floyd in the spring of 2020, he said this about the impact of racism and police brutality on the Black community. "I am not okay. I am not okay today. I want to give the Black community permission to say I am not okay. I am tired. I am tired. I have not watched the video of Ahmaud Arbery. It is too much. I have not watched the video of George Floyd. It is too much. Black people have to go to work the next day and be alright. I am not okay. I am tired. I am tired of racism."[1] Williams described Black fatigue. I define Black fatigue in chapter 2 as repeated variations of stress that result in extreme exhaustion and cause mental, physical, and spiritual maladies that are passed down from generation to generation.

The fatigue of enduring unrelenting racist systems was not new with the 2020 protests. What was new was that Black people from the famous to the everyday citizen were given "permission" to take off the proverbial muzzle to tell the world about their pain and rage without fear of the normal backlash (e.g., "Why do you people always play the race card?"). It seemed as if the world was finally willing to listen. Black people were no longer denying or suppressing the emotional toll. We were boldly and poignantly calling out the impact of living in a racist world and demanding actions that put more of the burden on white people to change racist systems. White people could no longer claim sublime ignorance.

Black people have been marching, protesting, resisting, writing, orating, praying, legislating, and commentating for centuries for equity and justice, and—young and old—we are fatigued. It is physically, mentally, and emotionally draining to continue to experience inequities and even atrocities day after day when justice, equity, and fairness are purportedly legislated rights of all citizens of these United States of America.

At the height of the 2020 protests, I facilitated many listening and learning sessions. I was asked to serve on several panels with CEOs and key leaders of organizations. These virtual town hall gatherings were usually open to all employees and often included Black panelists who shared personal stories.

Several times CEOs admitted that they did not know about the daily challenges of navigating life as a Black person. One CEO, whose chief financial officer is Black, said that he was embarrassed that he had known his CFO for many years and had no sense of the emotional toll he faced from living while Black.

This is what *Black Fatigue: How Racism Erodes the Mind, Body, and Spirit* is about. It is about the fatigue that comes from the pain and anguish of living with racism every single day of your life. It is about being fatigued by those who are surprised and express outrage (with no action) that such inequities still exist. It is about the constant fatigue of not knowing whether you or a loved will come home alive. It is about enduring the ravages of intergenerational racism.

I am a child of the 1960s. As the editor of my high school newspaper, I wrote about the ills of discrimination. I was also a writer for my college newspaper, where I wrote about racist behaviors and participated in rallies and marches protesting inequitable treatment. Essentially my whole career has been dedicated to diversity, equity, and inclusion work. And it is mind-bogglingly fatiguing to realize that not much has changed. I explore my Black fatigue in chapter 1.

The injustices that I write about in this book have been recounted over the centuries by great writers, politicians, theologians, educators, and, as important, everyday people who come into the limelight because of a lived experience that shocks and appalls us like George Floyd's or Eric Garner's or Sandra Bland's—that lets us all know that even though we might want to believe that we have overcome bigotry, injustice, hatred, and race-based violence, the sad truth is that it is not so. Systems of oppression continue to loom large; many race-based inequities are just as prevalent today as they were 400 years ago. In chapter 3, "Then *Is* Now," I chronicle the lack of progress in addressing racism in the United States.

While we might want to rest on our laurels on the progress from slavery to freedom to modern-day wins like the pinnacle achievement, the election of Barack Obama as president, I daresay those who throughout history fought for equal rights would not be satisfied, nor should we be. While we might want to congratulate ourselves for legislation that makes overt acts of racism illegal, they still happen too frequently and often continue to require more legal action to address racist practices. As a recent example of legislation, consider the CROWN Act, which protects the right of Black people to wear our hair in its natural state. Some 6 states and jurisdictions have passed the act, and 20 more states are considering it. The bill was also introduced to Congress for federal protection in 2019.[2] It is incomprehensible to think that we need a law to protect the right to wear our hair as we prefer—that such oppression still exists. It is indeed fatiguing to have to put energy into struggling for what on the surface seems like a laughable issue.

Black Fatigue is a research-informed narrative of the causes and consequences of Black fatigue. I chronicle my personal lived experiences and those of family, colleagues, and friends. It is chock full of historical data and stories that illuminate the woeful lack of progress in achieving socioeconomic, health, educational, voting rights, and criminal justice equity over the past three-plus centuries. Though some Black people have achieved mobility and access, even we are not exempt from anti-Black racism.

The book highlights the complexities of the interconnected, multilayered, compounding factors caused by racism that perpetuate the cycle of fatigue. As shown in figure Intro.1, navigating centuries-old racist systems leads to intergenerational stress and trauma, increasing inherited health disparities that manifest as generations of oppressively inequitable life experiences and outcomes for Black people. Many municipalities have declared racism a public health emergency.

Science has proved that racism is a direct cause of physiological and psychological maladies. Black people suffer disproportionately from diseases such as high blood pressure, heart disease, cancer, and obesity. Many of these health issues are uncorrelated to socioeconomic status. In other words, contrary to what might seem intuitive, education and income are not

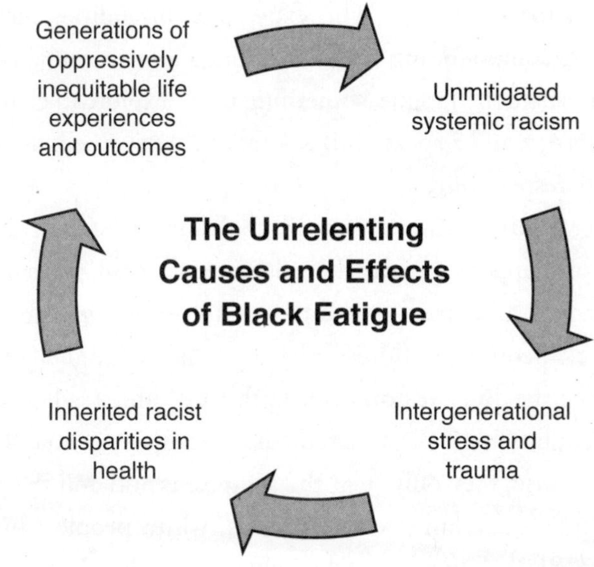

Figure Intro.1. The unrelenting causes and effects of Black fatigue
Source: author.

mitigators. Further, experts have recently made connections to how chronic stress affects us at the cellular level and is passed down generationally. Chapter 4 is devoted to exploring inequities in health outcomes.

While the title of the book is *Black Fatigue*, there are multiple layers that need consideration because of our intersectional identities. I am a cisgender, heterosexual Black woman who was born into the baby boom generation. My income puts me into the category of middle class. I am able-bodied. I have not been a victim of domestic violence, and I was raised in a two-parent household, albeit a lower-income one. My gender identity, sexual orientation, income, physical and mental status, and other social factors provide me privileges that Black people who are, for example, in the LGBTQ community, who are poor, who are subjected to violence, or who experience disabilities may not enjoy. The compounding stressors of one's intersectional identities exacerbate the fatigue, something that I explore in chapter 5. Chapters 6, 7, and 8 speak to Black fatigue for women, men, and children, respectively.

I offer solutions throughout the book and in detail in chapter 9. Racism happens at several levels: interpersonal, internalized, institutional, and structural. Intra- and interpersonal solutions for Black people to address racism-induced fatigue, such as resistance, healing, restoration, faith, rest, and resilience, are important but not end-game remedies because they do not solve the root cause; they only treat the symptoms and dull the pain.

On intra- and interpersonal levels, white people can help mitigate Black fatigue by acknowledging their whiteness and thus privilege, doing their own education on the history of racism, and becoming antiracist allies who challenge white supremacy. For those who may not understand what some of these terms mean, I define them in chapter 2.

At the institutional and structural levels, as a start, the United States needs to atone for slavery publicly and offer reparations to descendants of slaves. We also need those in power to abolish racist legislation, policies, and practices. It can be done quickly, as we witnessed during the 2020 racial protests. Within a two-week period, motions were filed in states and municipalities across the country to defund police departments, ban chokeholds and the use of tear gas, and update use-of-force rules. Some companies declared Juneteenth a paid holiday, and a handful of CEOs who showed themselves to be racist stepped down. Within weeks of receiving a request from a 22-year-old Black woman, the *Merriam-Webster* dictionary agreed to change the definition of "racism" to include the structural component. It should not have taken a global rebellion for racial justice to bring about these changes. However, it did, demonstrating that systems can be changed when those with the power choose to exercise it to dismantle white supremacist structures.

The corporate world needs to embrace more of a social justice rather than a merely capitalistic approach to what has become known as diversity, equity, and inclusion (DEI). We need diversity, equity, inclusion, and justice (DEIJ).

In chapter 9, I reimagine a decolonized world that bends toward racial justice. In that world, we would never see another Black person gunned down by law enforcement or anybody else solely on the basis of their race; Black people would truly feel, based on equitable treatment, as if we belong in our own country; we could count on all the systems to work just as well for Black people as they do for white people; we would focus on achieving equity, not equality; white people would no longer, on the one hand, appropriate our culture and, on the other, treat us as inferior beings; white people would understand that because white culture is "normal," it renders all others "abnormal" by default; white people would understand white supremacy and that it will end only when white people see it as a white issue rather than a Black issue that they empathize with; white people would heed Robin DiAngelo's advice and face their white fragility,[3] the defensiveness that often arises in discussions of race.

White people must address institutional and structural racism. Black people do not have the power to change white supremacist systems. Prolific writer and social activist for Black liberation James Baldwin called whites "the innocents" in an essay ("My Dungeon Shook") in the form of a letter to his nephew in *The Fire Next Time* in 1962. He asserted that white people, by and large, believe themselves to be absolved of any accountability for the racist systems that prevents Black liberation. "They [white people] are in effect still trapped in a history which they do not understand and until they understand it, they cannot be released from it."[4] He asserted that it was not the responsibility of Black people to fix racism. However, he held optimism that, working together, Black and white people could effect change. Baldwin died in 1987 without seeing his hope come to fruition. Sadly, some 30 years later, we still have not seen that hope realized. It is too soon to tell whether the 2020 Black Lives Matter movement for racial justice will lead to sustained change. I, like James Baldwin, am still hopeful.

Every white person in this country—I do not care what he says or what she says—knows one thing. . . . They know that they would not like to be Black here. If they know that, they know everything they need to know. And whatever else they may say is a lie.

—James Baldwin, Black novelist, essayist, playwright, poet, social critic, and one of America's foremost writers

ONE

My Black Fatigue

I was hard-pressed to name it. It is an underlying syndrome of sorts that permeates my very being. It operates like a dull droning sound that is always present but most of the time is drowned out by the higher pitches of my optimism and hope. I now know it to be Black fatigue.

In sharing my story, I relate experiences of individual racism that do not explicitly uncover the systems that undergird such examples and make them possible. Racism operates at the intrapersonal, interpersonal, institutional, and structural levels. It is often systemic racism that creates the day-to-day personal experiences that I share here and throughout the book.

The Early Years

My Black fatigue started when I was five years old. Of course, I did not know it then, but I now recognize how that incident affected me and the way I would interact with the world from then on. I was in kindergarten in 1956, just two years after the landmark *Brown v. Board of Education* decision banning segregated schools.[1] I was oblivious to all of that because I lived in the small town of Niagara Falls, New York, where the population was about 100,000 at that time and the Black population was probably no more than 10 percent. My school therefore was predominantly white. As a matter of fact, Karen (not her real name) and I were the only two Black children in the class. The ugliness of racism did not escape us.

One day Bobby (not his real name), a freckle-face white boy, called Karen and me the "*n*" word. We were not exactly sure what it meant, but we knew it was not nice, so we started crying. The teacher came to our rescue and inquired as to why we were crying. After we told her, she called Bobby into the coatroom and told him that his red hair was ugly, and his freckles were too. While I am not sure a child psychologist would have concurred with the teacher's approach, it worked for us because Bobby was crying now too.

This was the first time I really knew that I was different and that somebody would be mean to me because of it. Consider the impressionable minds of five-year-old children and the realization that skin color made Karen and me the subject of disdain. My parents tried to explain what the word meant and how it was used to denigrate "Negroes." (Yes, I am old enough that we were still referred to as Negroes.)

On that day, I changed from a carefree little girl to a cautious and insecure one, not being sure when somebody might be mean to me again because of the color of my skin. The realization that I might not be accepted by everyone—having to think about it and consider it—was and is stressful and contributes to Black fatigue.

It is not unusual for Black children to have life-transforming, aha! moments such as my kindergarten experience. Sometimes in our diversity learning sessions we ask the question, When was the first time you knew that you were different, and what did it feel like? It is not uncommon to hear from Black and other people of color that it was during participants' formative years (ages 5–10). Research shows that babies as young as six months old demonstrate a preference for their own race.[2]

It was not so much the specific name-calling as it was the realization that I was Black, different, not considered as good as, that was indelibly planted in my mind and that my parents could not make me feel better about. I think I knew I was Black; I just did not know the implications. You see, my parents were Canadians, and not that they did not have their stories of racist situations, but they did not have the US southern racial experience. Both of my parents' ancestors used the Underground Railroad to settle in Canada, and my mother loved her homeland much more than the United States, to the extent that she proudly carried her green card until the day she died at age 57. If she had lived, my parents were planning to go back to Canada after my father's retirement.

My dad did not talk much about race, but my mother told me that the reason they did not graduate from high school was that "colored" children were only expected to matriculate to grade 9. My dad was born in the United States and was raised by an uncle in Niagara Falls, Ontario, because his parents had died within months of each other from tuberculosis. He served in World War II in a segregated troop, married, and moved to the American side of the falls and worked as a laborer for DuPont for over 40 years.

My stark awareness of my race just continued to escalate after my kindergarten experience. My mother had cousins who lived in Baltimore, Maryland. We drove to visit them from time to time. Every time we crossed the Mason-Dixon line, my mother would turn to me in the back seat and say, "Now you have to be good. Be quiet and sit still." This was even before the police stopped us, which happened several times. They apparently saw the New York State license plates and a Black man behind the wheel and wondered what we were doing out of state. They always asked my dad, a very law-abiding, nondrinking, nonsmoking, pious Christian, "Where are you going?" I was so scared by these incidents that one time I even wet my pants. (I discuss the effects of race-based stress on children in chapter 8.) From the time I was five, being Black meant being on guard. As I read accounts from other authors who are writing about their early experiences with race, I find they are very similar to mine. So many Black and Brown people learned early that the color of our skin rather than their skin mattered in ways that frightened us not them and caused fear and stress.

Most of our vacations were spent in Canada with my mother's family. She wanted to visit as much as she could, so we spent most holidays and summer vacations in Owen Sound, Ontario, about 110 miles north of Toronto. My aunt Frances (after whom I am named) was quite an activist, fighting for civil rights for the Saugeen First Nation of Indians to reclaim their land. I did not understand it all then, but during our visits to Canada, she was often consumed with marches and developing petitions and other legal documents. There were plenty of discussions about racism in Canada at the dinner table with Aunt Frances, my parents, and my uncles.

Other than the informal family discussions, I really knew very little about Black history in grades K–7. There were only cursory mentions in elementary school books, if any. In middle school, my best friend, Alnita, wrote an essay on Sojourner Truth. Alnita was brilliant and a great writer. She had a way with words even in the seventh grade. She read her essay in class and even the teacher was speechless. Most students at that age would write about a famous person in a very sterile, biographical fashion, but Alnita's essay helped you to feel the pain and suffering, as well as the determination and audacity of Sojourner Truth. It was life changing for me for two reasons. First, I had never heard of Sojourner Truth, and second, I could not have conceived that there was a Black woman in the 1800s who challenged slavery and was an advocate for women's rights in such a fervent and visible way.

Alnita spurred my love of writing and my interest in Black history. I learned that the NAACP had its roots in Niagara Falls. The Niagara Movement was a civil rights group founded in 1905 in Niagara Falls, Ontario. Scholar and activist W. E. B. Du Bois gathered with a small group of supporters on the Canadian side because they could not stay in hotels on the American side. The purpose of this meeting was to form an organization dedicated to social and political change for Black people in the United States. The group put together demands that included an end to segregation and discrimination in unions, the courts, and public accommodations, as well as equality of economic and educational opportunity. While the Niagara Movement had little impact on legislative action, it led to the formation of the National Association for the Advancement of Colored People (NAACP) in 1909.[3] Learning this bit of history about my region was truly exciting and motivated me to keep digging.

In high school, I was the editor of the school newspaper. This was the late 1960s and the civil rights movement was in full swing. I was writing about Martin Luther King Jr., Malcom X (that piece was banned because of the widespread negative perception of him at that time), women's rights, the Vietnam War, and other social issues of the day. More times than not, my pieces were edited by the teacher who oversaw the newspaper because she thought them to be too controversial. It was frustrating and fatiguing to be censured.

In my senior year of high school, after I was accepted to the University of Rochester, my guidance counselor suggested that perhaps that school was too lofty a goal for someone like me. Sorry, my bags were packed. I was going and I was going to show her (another stressor, feeling I needed to prove myself). When I arrived at the university, there were 69 Black students (the previous year there were only 10) out of a student body of about 5,000 undergraduates. There was a two-tier set of admissions criteria for students of color—Equal Opportunity Program and "regular admits." I was a regular admit, meaning I did not have to attend the summer program designed to acclimate students of color to the university, but I was painfully aware that all of my professors assumed I was a part of the Equal Opportunity Program, and there were clear biases and signals that I/we did not belong. Regardless of my admission status, I know that it was because of affirmative action that I received a full scholarship to the university. My parents surely would not have been able to afford the tuition. I am proud to proclaim that I benefited from affirmative action. Without it, I know that I would not be where I am today.

The president of the university at the time said something to the effect that he thought most Black students would do better at the community college. The Black Student Union took over the administration building, demanding a retraction. I was a part of that takeover. As a matter of fact, we held many demonstrations and late-night meetings to bring light to the discriminatory behaviors that we were constantly subjected to, such as security officers questioning whether the students of color were really enrolled at the university. Sound familiar? In 2018 a white student called the police to report that a Black female was sleeping in a common area of a dorm at Yale University. The white student was concerned that she did not belong there, and it made her uncomfortable.[4] It was fatiguing to have to justify one's existence while attempting to concentrate on schoolwork.

Adding to my Black history acumen, upon arrival at the University of Rochester, I learned that Frederick Douglass and Harriet Tubman had run abolitionist movement activities in Rochester, New York. Douglass printed his *North Star* newspaper in the city, and Rochester was a part of the Underground Railroad. Douglass is buried in the Mount Hope Cemetery, which is adjacent to the campus.[5] One Halloween a group of students decided to try to find his marker. I cannot even describe the feeling of knowing that these great freedom fighters walked the same ground as me.

While my undergraduate days were fun, the racism was truly exhausting and affected my ability to always be attentive to my classes.

Fifteen years after obtaining my bachelor's degree and MBA from the university, I was elected as the first African American female trustee. During my time as a voting trustee, it was fatiguing to be the only Black person at many meetings and to continually point out the lack of diversity at all levels of the university and watch my concerns be minimized or dismissed. This is not meant as an indictment of the university; I am sharing my experience. It is the history of many universities in this country. The higher-education system has not changed since my days as a student or a trustee. Chapter 3 provides a then-and-now portrait of diversity in a number of aspects of society. The lack of progress is fatiguing.

The Work World

I started my work career in 1973, and affirmative action helped to jump-start it. The Eastman Kodak Company, along with most *Fortune* 100 companies at the time, was scrambling to comply with the Civil Rights Act of 1964 and Executive Order 11246, which was signed into law in 1965 and required not only nondiscrimination in employment but also affirmative action. I was hired into a management rotational program and landed in the affirmative action department. My job was to defend the company against discrimination complaints. Working with outside attorneys, I wrote "position papers." Fresh out of undergraduate school with degrees in psychology and English, I felt woefully underqualified for the task. However, I was the token Black person that the company could showcase. There was really no one else of color at a higher level to take on this role. It was stressful and fatiguing because of the learning curve and feeling out of my element but also because I did not always believe that the company had not discriminated against the individual, or individuals in the case of class action suits.

A few years later I was one of four "high-potential" employees selected for the executive MBA program at the University of Rochester. The three others were white men who were all promoted to vice president roles after graduation. I, on the other hand, was asked what I wanted to do. I immediately selected a high-level role, since my classmates had been appointed to such positions. I was told by the head of HR that no such role was contemplated for me at that time. I was assigned to competitive intelligence in marketing. It was a new department (Kodak did not formalize a competitive process until the mid-1980s), and they thought it would be a good move for me. I was assigned to study Fuji, Kodak's archrival. It was before the advent of the World Wide Web, so I had to do my research the old-fashioned way—library and LexisNexis.

I worked for six months on the Fuji presentation for the executive team. Proud of my super sleuthing skills and confident that this presentation would be my ticket to a management position, I made my presentation. I basically told leadership that Fuji would be a formidable competitor. It had plans to penetrate the US market. I was asked to leave after my presentation while my boss stayed behind (I did not rank high enough to hear the after-discussion). When he returned to the office, he did not look happy. He said that he had to fight for me to keep my job. The executive team did not believe my findings. They did not think Fuji was such a threat—they believed that I had sensationalized the presentation. I was shocked. Well, not to brag, but I was right. The Fuji blimp appeared in US skies the next year, Kodak lost the advertising bid for the Olympics to Fuji, and the rest, shall we say, is history. I do not know for sure why my assessment was not deemed credible; I can only assume that who I was contributed to their reaction. It was stressful and fatiguing.

The whole time I was in the corporate world, I did not know how to be. I had bosses who told me I was too aggressive and others who told me I was not aggressive enough. While sporting a short Afro hair style, I was asked whether my hair would grow. When I said yes, I was told that I should let it because the Afro was not professional. (Black women's natural hair is still an issue today, as discussed in chapter 6.) The stress of not knowing who to be or how to show up so that I would be accepted led me to leave the corporate world to start my own business.

It was fatiguing to be tokenized, be discredited, and not be allowed to bring even half of myself into the workplace. The microaggressions (I will elaborate on them in chapter 6) were so common that I think I became hardened to them. I was miserable and often went home and cried about these experiences in the arms of my very supportive late husband, Joe, whom I talk about later in the chapter. The straw that broke the proverbial camel's back for me was when I had a blatant sexual harassment experience. I remained silent, but I could no longer stay in that environment. I was fatigued.

While my experiences in the corporate world happened over 30 years ago, I continue to hear the very same stories from young Black professionals today.

As you are reading this, you might be thinking, It seems like you did OK. Affirmative action worked for you. And there is no denying that it did. This is an example of a federal policy that enabled thousands of people of color at lower socioeconomic levels to go to college. Programs inspired by affirmative action are still helping people who would not otherwise be able to attain the education they need to enhance their chances to achieve their life's goals. While data show that white women have been the primary beneficiaries of affirmative action,[6] people of color have also benefited, albeit to a lesser degree. And many of these programs are being rolled back under the Trump administration as unfair to white students. The Trump administration called for abandoning Obama administration policies that allowed universities to consider race as a factor in diversifying their campuses.[7] This is a prime example of "two steps forward and three steps backward." It is fatiguing to have to continue to fight for affirmative action—a policy signed into law in 1965. It is fatiguing not to be able to have confidence that gains made based on such programs are sustainable.

Living While Black

As I researched and wrote chapter 4, "Racism Literally Makes You Sick," memories of my late husband, Joseph Winters, were in my mind. He, like me, was a first-generation college graduate, coming from urban Washington, DC, in the 1960s. He had a degree in statistics and an MBA and worked as a director of finance for Eastman Kodak. He died of a massive heart attack in 1997, at age 47. He was diagnosed with coronary artery disease at age 38, after months of not feeling well and having no tests performed to explore the possibility that his shortness of breath and chest pain were related to his heart. When he was finally diagnosed, the cardiologist said that he had suffered a heart attack several months before; there was now significant heart damage and he needed a transplant. In the meantime, we found a renowned heart surgeon who was willing to perform quintuple bypass surgery in lieu of a transplant, which he really could not wait for. He lived for nine years after the surgery. There were no strong hereditary markers for heart disease in his family. I cannot be sure whether the stress of being one of a few Black men at his level in a major corporation contributed to his heart disease. I cannot be sure that, had he been diagnosed sooner, the outcome would have been any different. I cannot be sure that the reason he was not diagnosed sooner was related to racism. It is something I still wonder about.

Joe and I produced two amazing offspring. Joe II is the tenured Alexander F. Hehmeyer Associate Professor of Religious Studies and African and African American Studies with secondary positions in English and gender, sexuality, and feminist studies at Duke University, and our daughter, Mareisha, is trained as an electrical engineer but left the field as a result of many of the same inequities that I encountered and that other women in STEM fields face. She has served as chief operating officer at The Winters Group for the last eight years. She has been instrumental in the company's double-digit growth.

When Joe was 13, I came home from work one day to find a police car in the driveway with my son in the back seat. I was very surprised and concerned. Joe was a straight-A, mild-mannered young man and certainly never in trouble. The police officer informed me that a parent of another student had filed a complaint that Joe had started a fight with the boy on the bus. After receiving more information, I learned that the other boy (white) had been bullying my son for weeks. This account was corroborated by other students. The other boy challenged my son to a fight. According to my son, the fight lasted all of five seconds, and the other kid had a minor injury. I would have thought that the other parent might have contacted me or Joe's dad instead of calling the police. The police officer found Joe at a neighbor's house playing basketball. He apparently had to search the suburban neighborhood, and my son would stand out as the only Black boy. Joe was afraid, and so was I. When his dad got home from work, we had the "talk," which I explain in chapter 8. It is not uncommon for spontaneous thoughts about his safety to still manifest for no apparent reason. That incident happened almost 30 years ago, and we know that it could have just as easily been today.

When Mareisha was 10, she begged for a dog. No one else in the family really wanted a dog. We finally gave in, and on her eleventh birthday we surprised her with a little brown-and-white shih tzu. He was too young to leave his mother, so we eagerly anticipated his arrival in six weeks' time. Two weeks before we were to pick up Snickers, as he had been so named by Mareisha, I received a call from the breeder. She said that we could no longer have the dog. I was shocked. I could not imagine why. After doing some checking with the person who connected us with the breeder, we learned that the breeder's partner had discovered that we were Black and refused to sell us the dog. There was no way that I was going to tell an 11-year-old child that she could not have a dog because she is Black, so I immediately went searching for a dog that looked like Snickers. I found one, but the process was stressful and fatiguing. I tried to find some organization that would address this blatant racism. It seems that because she was an independent breeder, there was little recourse.

Again, the sad part is that this happened almost 30 years ago but could just as easily have happened last week.

CHAPTER ONE

In My Work

After almost four decades in the diversity, equity, and inclusion business, there are thousands of stories that I might share. I have selected one that happened in the course of writing this book that epitomizes the reason for Black fatigue: a failure on the part of many white people to "get it"—to get how their white identity represents the normalized dominant culture and abnormalizes every other identity.

As part of a large professional services firm's multicultural summit, I was asked to be a breakout speaker on white culture and inclusion in the workplace. In another breakout session, the Center for Talent Innovation presented the findings of its most recent research on Black professionals in the workplace. The first thing I noticed was that even though the summit of over 350 people was very visually diverse, the Center for Talent Innovation breakout session of over 50 people was attended by only Black people, with the exception of two whites. My session on white culture was also attended primarily by Black, Latino, and Asian participants.

In my experience presenting at and attending many conferences over the years, sessions on topics pertaining to Black people are almost always filled primarily with Black people. We refer to this phenomenon as "preaching to the choir." After such sessions, attendees may feel affirmed by the opportunity to share common experiences, but they also likely feel frustrated with the recounting of the lack of progress. In the case of the Center for Talent Innovation study of over 3,000 respondents, there were many data points that confirmed lack of progress, such as the fact that black professionals hold only 3.2 percent of all executive or senior leadership roles and less than 1 percent of all *Fortune*

500 CEO positions, even though we represent 12 percent of the workforce.

In my session on white culture, well-meaning white people in the room were hard-pressed to know what to do, even though they were interested in the topic. I shared whiteness theory concepts based on scholarly research that shows that many white people see themselves as "raceless and cultureless." A study by Pew Research conducted in 2019 revealed that 75 percent of Blacks and over 50 percent of Latinx and Asians regard their racial identity as very important to them, while only 15 percent of whites responded that their racial identity was important.[8] One of the young white men in the room said, "It's true. My race is not important. If it is not, how can I make it? I can't feel something that I just don't." I recommended that he start reading about the history of white people and whiteness theory to get more grounded in the ideas. I suggest some specific references in chapter 2. While most of the participants of color were eager to support this young man's learning, there were a few eyes rolling like, Really? The sentiment voiced by a few was, "I don't want to be your teacher, and you should know what to do."

It is fatiguing for me after all these years to hear about the same lack of progress toward racial equity decade after decade and have white people respond with the same ignorance or lack of interest in the topic or by not acknowledging the profound impact of their racial identity. I sometimes do not know whether to scream, cry, or just give up.

SUMMARY

Even with all the fatiguing experiences I have encountered because I am Black, I am blessed. I benefited from the early affirmative action days when the powers that be were afraid and wanted to avoid lawsuits. Even though I was the token in many instances, it has likely been a lot easier for me than for other people of color who did not get that boost. I know that I had to work at least twice as hard to get where I am, and I am fatigued. However, I want to bring hope to the generations that now hold the torch. When I hear millennials declare that they are exhausted and not willing to be the educators of the ignorant, I am gravely concerned. The inequitable systems will continue to be exhausting for millennials and Generation Z (born after 1997) to navigate, whether they are teachers or not. Black fatigue leads to all manner of physical and emotional problems, many of which go undetected. Lifting the burden of being an educator may lessen the day-to-day fatigue, but that alone will not dismantle racist systems. As I shared in the introduction, maybe the 2020 global Black Lives Matter protests against racism were a real wake-up call. No longer could white people claim sublime ignorance of anti-Black racism.

It is certain, in any case, that ignorance, allied with power, is the most ferocious enemy justice can have.

—James Baldwin, Black novelist, essayist, playwright, poet, social critic, and one of America's foremost writers

TWO
Addressing Sublime Ignorance

"I just didn't know," opined corporate leaders during the wake of the 2020 Black Lives Matter rebellions against racism. They claimed they did not know that racism affected Black people so deeply. Now that we know, many vowed, we are committed to addressing systemic racism.

This was not the first time I had heard the embarrassed admission from top brass that they were not aware of the day-to-day racism that the Black employees face. Randall Stephenson, AT&T's CEO, addressed the employee resources groups in 2016, after incidents of police shootings in several cities, including the widely publicized killing of Michael Brown, an unarmed Black teen, in Ferguson, Missouri in 2014. In a video that went viral, Stephenson, a white man, vulnerably and sincerely admitted his ignorance about racism to the group. He recounted a story of his Black friend of 30 years, a medical doctor, who had shared a video with Stephenson of a talk he had given at his church. In the talk, the doctor outlined incidents of being stopped by police, being called "boy," being mistaken for a server in restaurants, and never forgetting to carry ID when jogging in his neighborhood. Stephenson said that he was shocked by his friend's story and embarrassed that after such a long and close relationship, he had no idea how racism shaped the doctor's daily lived experiences. The doctor's story is all too familiar to many Black people.

This is what I call sublime (defined as "elevated and exalted") ignorance. When many Black people hear stories like this, we do not know whether to scream, cry, or laugh. How could you not know that racism is alive and well in America and throughout the world? The truth is that white people are not required to know. As the dominant group, they can go through life with the privilege of never thinking about their race. Many white people still claim not to "see" race. If you do not see it, there is no reason to address it. You can be sublimely ignorant. Many admit that they do not know the history of racism in this country. Most K–12 history books gloss over, sanitize, or inaccurately portray the realities of racism, and if you do not "see" race, why would you take the initiative to study it? If you want to be antiracist, you need to have the knowledge. I refer you to some excellent resources, such as Ibram X. Kendi's *Stamped from the Beginning*,[1] which was written to tell the true story of the history of racist systems in America. The 1619 Project is an ongoing project of the New York Times created by Nikole Hannah Jones, to re-examine the legacy of slavery.[2] Carol Anderson's *White Rage*[3] chronicles the history of the entrenched forces that keep racism alive because of white anger and resentment. *Black*

Reconstruction in America[4] by W. E. B. Du Bois, *The Slave Ship: A Human History*[5] by Marcus Rediker, *A People's History of the United States*[6] by Howard Zinn, and *The History of White People*[7] by Nell Irvin Painter all recount history from the perspective of those who have been oppressed, challenging some of the accounts in traditional textbooks.

Every client The Winters Group has ever had boasts that it is data driven and its leaders respond to statistics and facts. There is no shortage of data to prove that anti-Black racism is, in many cases, just as prevalent today as it was 400 years ago. I expound on current inequities in chapter 3. Why is it that it took global antiracism Black Lives Matter rebellions to wake the world up to these injustices? Those of us who are in the business of diversity, equity, inclusion, and justice, have been trying to get the attention of corporate leaders for decades, only to be met with resistance or denial that racism against Black people was still a key concern. "Let's not make this about race. There are many other diversity dimensions that we need also consider." If I had a dollar for each time I heard that, I would be a wealthy woman.

I am surprised (perhaps I should not be) by the questions I get from participants in various sessions on diversity and race. The questions often show ignorance of common concepts. The activists of this new movement are making it clear that it is not our job to educate the sublimely ignorant. One way to lessen the emotional toll and fatigue on Black people is for the sublimely innocent to do their own work.

Having said that, this book is a part of the education. If you are reading it, you are doing the work of educating yourself. In this chapter, I offer definitions and clarifications of some key concepts that may be new, especially to people in the corporate world. In the corporate arena, concepts like diversity, equity, inclusion, and belonging are more popular than the terms that I define in this chapter, such as "racism," "white supremacy," and "decolonization." "Diversity" refers to the representation of different demographic groups in the organization. "Inclusion" and "belonging" are closely related and refer to the action of creating work environments that respect and value the differences. "Equity" is defined shortly.

The Winters Group studies the intersection of corporate diversity and inclusion work and social justice equity approaches. To understand and address Black fatigue, it is necessary to grasp these concepts aimed at dismantling systemic racism. Corporate diversity efforts have failed to solve the systemic practices and policies that perpetuate inequitable outcomes, such as a lack of visibly diverse representation in senior leadership positions. I posit that the reason for this is that the rationale for corporate diversity focuses more on the "business case" than on social justice. The business case sounds like this: "Diversity drives innovation"; "Having more women in the C-suite drives profits"; "Diversity provides more opportunities to sell products to multicultural consumers." In corporate spheres, we have mastered capitalistic language for "It is the right thing to do for business" but shy away from ideas that get to the structural, historical isms that would support "It is the just thing to do." Using the business case as the primary rationale for diversity can be exploitative—hiring Black people will yield more profit.

Understanding social justice concepts will provide new ways of addressing diversity, equity, and inclusion (DEI) efforts with a racial justice lens. I call this intersection diversity, equity, inclusion, and justice (DEIJ).

Black Fatigue

I should first define what I mean by "Black fatigue." The dictionary defines "fatigue" as extreme tiredness resulting from mental or physical exertion or illness. A secondary definition refers to metal fatigue, weakness in materials, especially metal, caused by repeated variations of stress. While the second definition is not related to human fatigue, I think it is apropos, especially the cause—repeated variations of stress. Therefore, I define "Black fatigue" as repeated variations of stress that result in extreme exhaustion and cause mental, physical, and spiritual maladies that are passed down from generation to generation. It is a deeply embedded fatigue that takes inordinate amounts of energy to overcome—herculean efforts to sustain an optimistic outlook and enormous amounts of faith to continue to believe "we shall overcome someday." Repeatedly, I hear a resounding chorus from Black people I work with as I go from company to company consulting on DEIJ: "We are exhausted."

Race

For those who deny race, let me share its meaning and manifestation. Race is a social construct developed by dominant groups to categorize people by physical characteristics, mainly skin color. While there is no biological basis for these distinctions, those who identify or were identified by whites as Black have been considered inferior to those labeled as white. Still today, inequitable systems carry out this belief through racist practices. As I said earlier, complicating the definition of race is the fact that many white people have been socialized not to "see" race, especially their own, which leads to ignorance and denial of racial differences. As mentioned in chapter 1, only 15 percent of whites think their race is important to their identity. Until more white people acknowledge that race matters—that "white" as a racial classification really matters—we will continue to be stalled in our progress. White people must acknowledge their whiteness. If there were no white, there would be no Black, and vice versa.

We need to get comfortable talking about race and racism and stop using our discomfort as an excuse not to. It only serves to perpetuate and accept sublime ignorance. Read *We Can't Talk About That at Work!*[8] and *Inclusive Conversations*[9] for strategies for talking about race.

Equity versus Equality

"Equity" can be defined as the treatment of people according to what they need and deserve. This is contrasted with the more familiar term "equality," which connotes that we treat everybody the same.

There is a popular image showing three children trying to view a baseball game over a fence. In the first picture in figure 2.1, each child is standing on the same size box. However, the tallest child does not need a box, and the smallest child still cannot see because the box is not high enough to accommodate her needs. In the first picture, each child is treated equally but not equitably. In the second picture, equity, the three boxes have been reallocated so that the smallest child is given two boxes, the next-smallest child is given one because that is what he needs, and the tallest child is not provided with a box because he can see over the fence without it. The third image, liberation, shows the barrier (fence) completely removed. Removing barriers is the ultimate goal.

Figure 2.1. Equality, equity, liberation
Source: The Winters Group, Inc. Art by Krystle Nicholas.

One client spent almost a year trying to convince the organization that it should add equity to its diversity and inclusion strategy. Other clients have admitted that they are still trying to define diversity and inclusion and are clearly not ready to introduce the concept of equity. If organizations cannot include equity as one of their goals, what, then, is the goal?

Racist/Racism

Many people still believe that racism is something that only happens interpersonally, not recognizing that while it does happen at the individual level, it is more insidious as a set of systems and structures that favor the dominant group (mostly whites) and negatively affect subordinated groups. Racism involves one group having the power to carry out systematic discrimination through institutional policies and practices. Similarly, we are uncomfortable with the term "racist." Calling someone racist has become akin to alleging that they are a despicable person. And there is a difference between being nonracist and being antiracist. A nonracist is a person who has an inactive, passive belief that racism is wrong. It is one who rejects racism. Antiracists take a stand in their sphere of influence to oppose racism. For example, a nonracist might not tell a racist joke but would not intervene when someone else did. Perhaps the nonracist would even laugh along with others. An antiracist would not laugh at the joke and would go one step further to let the person know that the joke was inappropriate and offensive.

Some theorists believe that, at the core, we are all racists because we are part of a society whose very foundation was built on racist ideals and practices that persist today. Brain science reveals that we internalize racist messages from a racist society that become part of who we are—whether we are aware of it or not. Unless we are willing to acknowledge these realities and begin to use the term, we cannot address the racist systems that undergird our organizational practices. I know that corporations do not like to use this term because of the legal risks of admitting to racism. Notwithstanding that very valid concern, we must be willing to learn more about the history of racist systems that may still unwittingly drive processes and practices. We have to say the word to address the problem.

Most of the day-to-day accounts of racism convey individual-level racism and often fail to acknowledge the systems that undergird the issues. For example, we see media coverage of individual Blacks being exonerated after being incarcerated for crimes that they did not commit, and think these are isolated instances. However, there is a much bigger system of mass incarceration that disproportionately affects Black people, which Michelle Alexander portrays in her book *The New Jim Crow*.[10]

John McWhorter, professor at Columbia University and contributor to the *Atlantic*, penned a piece in July 2019[11] that posits that the definition of "racist" has morphed over the years. He says that the term "racist" has become synonymous with "evil," with almost the same emotional trigger as calling someone a pedophile. He believes that the power of the word carries as much weight in its "moral sanction" as the definition itself, meaning that if a critical mass does not think what was said was racist, then it cannot be so. One example he uses is President Donald Trump's admonition that the "Squad" (women of color House of Representative members Alexandria Ocasio-Cortez, IIhan Omar, Ayanna Pressley, and Rashida Tlaib) should all go back where they came from if they had criticism of the United States. All but one were born in the United States, and the other has lived in the United States for a long time. Trump's fellow Republicans loudly and proudly declared that the president was not a racist (morally that would clearly not be acceptable), and therefore his comments could not be deemed racist. This is an example of how dominant group power works. Narratives that advantage them are accepted by the rest of the dominant group.

Individuals can be considered racist if they believe, in general, that their group is superior to other groups and they have a history of consistently and publicly saying and acting in ways that would confirm their convictions. There is also misunderstanding on the question of whether Black people can be racists. The answer is yes and no. At the individual and interpersonal levels, we can harbor racist views of other groups. We have seen instances of Black people being anti-Semitic. Intragroup racism is an aspect of internalized oppression where you hate people who look like you. Most critical race theorists assert that Black people cannot be racist using the structural definition, as it necessitates having the power to implement policies that negatively affect subordinated groups and Black people do not collectively possess such power.

Nonracist versus Antiracist

In the book *How to Be Less Stupid about Race*, Crystal Fleming, a sociology professor at Stony Brook University, says nonracists think racism plays out as extreme, overt acts, such as hate crimes.[12] Nonracists might proudly declare, "I do not have a racist bone in my body," not understanding the entrenched structural nature of racism. Historian Ibram X. Kendi, author of *How to Be an Anti-racist*, said in a 2019 interview for the *Guardian*, "Proclaiming that you are 'not racist' does not require anyone to consider how they should fight racism."[13] It is not enough to not be racist; it's important to be opposed to racism and demonstrate such opposition in your words, deeds, and actions. Antiracists do not sit on the sidelines and say, "Isn't that awful," when they see racist actions. Antiracists take a stand in their sphere of influence to oppose racism.

White/Whiteness

Whiteness is normalized in culture, creating an unawareness of the set of privileges associated with white identity, also known as white privilege. Whiteness theory posits that whiteness is the default of American culture, and as a result, white people cannot see the advantages of being white—so much so that many do not even want to discuss whiteness. In many sessions that I conduct, white people express extreme discomfort in talking about whiteness or any aspect of racial dynamics. As pointed out earlier, only 15 percent of white people say that their race is core to their identity. White people must engage in honest self-reflection regarding the messages, images, values, beliefs, and experiences they have encountered living in a culture that continues to prioritize their worldviews as the better ones.

White Privilege

"White privilege" is defined as rights that only some people have access to as members of a dominant social group. Intragroup hierarchies of privilege exist, with people who are part of the group in power at the top (white or Caucasian people with respect to people of color, men with respect to women, heterosexuals with respect to homosexuals, adults with respect to children, and rich people with respect to poor people). White people often deny that their race affords them privilege. I have heard white people say, "I grew up poor and certainly was not privileged." On the dimension of wealth, perhaps not; however, racial privilege still exists. The key point is that people who are visibly "white" in complexion enjoy unearned privilege that, for the most part, they are oblivious to (sublime ignorance), unless they are intentional about understanding it. This oblivion or denial that such privilege exists is fatiguing for Black people. We cannot have meaningful discussions about addressing racism until there is understanding and acknowledgment of privilege. As an example, white parents do not have to have the "talk" that Black parents have with their children about how to respond if they are stopped by police. I explain the "talk" more in chapter 8.

White Supremacy

This is a term that is really misunderstood. When people hear "white supremacy," they think Ku Klux Klan, neo-Nazis, white nationalists, and avowed hate groups. While these groups openly admit their hatred for Blacks, Jewish people, immigrants, and so on and are prone to perpetrating violence against them based on their beliefs that whites are superior and all others should be eliminated, they by no means embody the definition of white supremacy.

White supremacy is the ideology, whether conscious or unconscious—explicit or implied—that white people and the ideas, thoughts, beliefs, and actions of white people are superior to people of color and their ideas, thoughts, beliefs, and actions.[14] It can also be defined as a political or socioeconomic system in which white people enjoy structural advantage and rights that other racial and ethnic groups do not, at both a collective and an individual level. White supremacy means that white ideals are the norm and, by default, every other group's beliefs are abnormal. Just as the term "supreme" conveys, whiteness is "superior" to all others.

In the corporate world, white supremacy is most often demonstrated as heterosexual white male supremacy. For example, organizational cultures are built to favor capitalism, individualism, and the "right to comfort" and entitlement. As I mentioned earlier, the rationale for diversity often comes from a capitalistic mind-set: "We are only interested in diversity if it benefits what we prioritize—profits." Individualism assumes that success is based solely on hard work without considering systemic barriers. The right to comfort may be expressed as not wanting to talk about race because it makes white people uncomfortable. There is comfort in perpetuating the idea of a color-blind world.

One of my clients shared a story that exemplifies what white supremacist ideology looks like. He attended a community meeting to discuss racism. He said there were probably 60 people at the meeting; 40 were Black and 20 white. He observed that the white people dominated the conversation, sharing their perceptions of how to address racism without giving equal voice to the Black participants. He said it finally hit him that white people just think it is normal to be in control of everything and to be experts on racism, even while admitting they don't know much about it.

Dominant and Subordinated Groups

Dominant and subordinated groups are another way to understand white supremacy. Dominant groups are those with systemic power, privileges, and social status within a society, most often white people. Conversely, subordinated groups are those that have been traditionally oppressed, excluded, or disadvantaged in society, most often Black and Brown people, Indigenous people, women, and members of the LGBTQ community (for the purposes of this book, I focus on Black people). Dominant groups are considered the norm and, by default, subordinated groups are considered "abnormal"; dominant groups make the rules, and all others are judged by their standards. Dominant and subordinated groups are not equivalent to the majority and the minority. Consider apartheid in South Africa. Blacks were the numerical majority; even so, whites were the dominant group with the power. Note that I use the term "subordinat*ed*" rather than "subordinat*e*." The very term "subordinate" suggests inferior. "Subordinat*ed*" is more accurate, as it denotes that the lesser status has been imposed.

Oppression

Subordination leads to oppression, defined as the systematic subjugation of one social group by a more powerful social group for the social, economic, and political benefit of the more powerful social group. Rita Hardiman and Bailey Jackson state that oppression exists when the following four conditions are present: (1) the oppressor group has the power to define reality for themselves and others, (2) the target groups take in and internalize the negative messages about them and end up cooperating with the oppressors (commonly known as internalized oppression), (3) genocide, harassment, and discrimination are so systemic and institutionalized that individuals are not necessary to keep it going, and (4) members of both the oppressor and target groups are socialized to play their roles as normal and correct.[15]

I have observed oppressive systems in organizations that purport to want to create inclusive environments. The diversity office is often woefully underresourced to achieve the goals that are set forth. The oppressor group, in this case top leadership, defines the reality—the diversity office does not need resources to do its job; the diversity officer cooperates with the oppressor, which leads to Black fatigue.

This is the story of a very well-respected chief diversity officer (CDO) in a *Fortune* 500 organization:

> As a CDO, I am always pounding my head against the wall, unable to have real and sustainable impact on our organizations. I have served in this role in three organizations and, in each instance, the senior-most leaders have convinced me that they wanted to advance D&I [diversity and inclusion] in their organizations and lured me in. Yet after about six months in the job, the honeymoon has consistently been over.

> Those budget dollars you are promised never come. You don't have a seat at the tables where critical business and people decisions are being made, your recommendations for policy and practice changes are often ignored, and your work is always an afterthought. Once you bring to leadership's attention the issues you have uncovered and the work that needs to be done to move forward, they get defensive and consistently push back, demanding more and more data and empirical proof that the experiences of their underrepresented recruits and professionals are real. . . . In the meantime, the underrepresented professionals in your organization are looking to you as their savior and are convinced you are going to save the day for them. Little do they know that you cannot! This conundrum has me very weary and I have become more pessimistic than I ever thought I would be. My days in this work are quickly coming to an end as I realize that it is killing my very spirit—I refuse to continue banging my head against the wall.

I have worked with this CDO, and she has been forced to play her role as "normal and correct." She has shared with me a number of times how fatiguing this role is and even admitted to "being on the edge" at times.

Social Justice

"Social justice" is a term that, until recently, we rarely heard in the corporate world, except in philanthropy conversations.

Social justice means the way in which human rights are experienced in the everyday lives of people at every level of society and the fair distribution of wealth, opportunities, and privileges. Persistent gender wage inequities are a matter of social justice. As it was not a term that was widely used in corporate venues until the Black Lives Matter protests of 2020, I received many questions about what it means.

As another example of white supremacy, several white participants in sessions challenged their organizations on moving in this direction, asserting that they objected to the idea of "redistribution" of resources. It was not fair to hardworking white people. Integrating a social justice lens with traditional DEI (DEIJ) efforts will not be without controversy.

Decolonization

"To decolonize" means to free a group from the oppressive powers of domination. I honor the genesis term "decolonize" in its historical and literal meaning that signifies the repatriation and return of land to the Indigenous communities from whom that land was originally stolen. Many of us continue to live on and benefit from colonization, and this needs to be acknowledged and understood. I do not want to misappropriate the term. However, I include it here because you will be hearing it used more by social justice advocates. In social justice parlance, decolonization is about undoing white supremacist structures that disadvantage Black people and other marginalized groups. The 2020 Black Lives Matter movement is an example of decolonization efforts, as well as attempts to defund police departments that intentionally engaged in violence against Black people. Colonization is also a state of mind when we contribute to and perpetuate colonial principles. "Decolonization of the mind" refers to active resistance of "settler state" norms and resurgence of precolonial Indigenous practices such as natural healing practices and "we" (collectivist) instead of "I" (individualistic) culture. In DEI work, decolonization might look like the following:

- Centering justice, humanity, and the dismantling of racist systems over the "business case" and profit in DEIJ strategies.
- Understanding and embracing, rather than avoiding and sanitizing, certain language and concepts that are critical to understanding equity and justice, such as those outlined in this chapter.
- Decentering white comfort over necessary change. Corporate DEI leaders spend inordinate amounts of time on efforts to make the white leaders comfortable.
- Promoting white allyship and shared risk.
- Placing greater emphasis on healing and managing the emotional fatigue associated with being in this work and holding marginalized identities.
- Understanding ourselves as being part of a much broader social change ecosystem, and how that should influence how we use our power (e.g., how we spend our money and with whom we partner in this work).

SUMMARY

There is a lot of work to do to combat sublime ignorance, and it starts with having a deep understanding of racism and its devastating impacts. It requires embracing a new lexicon that puts justice in the DEI equation—DEIJ. To do so, there is a lot to learn, unlearn, and relearn. This book will provide you with the reasons for Black fatigue; how it manifests differently for women, men, those with intersectional identities, and children; and what we can do about it.

The past is all that makes the present coherent.

—James Baldwin

THREE
Then *Is* Now

Early in the COVID-19 pandemic outbreak of 2020, reports that Black people were two to four times more likely to die from the disease[1] than white people were met with surprise. I was surprised by the surprise voiced by politicians and other leaders because health disparities among Black people are well researched and, I thought, well known. I discuss health disparities in depth in chapter 4. This is another example of sublime ignorance.

Not only do many, especially white people, not know much about racist systems that disproportionately affect Black people, they also seem to be unaware of the lack of progress in reversing the trends. This is a major source of fatigue for Black people. There has been a lack of significant progress since legislation such as the *Brown v. Board of Education* Supreme Court decision of 1954 ending segregated public schools; the Civil Rights Act of 1964 banning segregation in public places and discrimination in hiring; Voting Rights Act of 1965 guaranteeing what had been promised in the Fifteenth Amendment; and the federal Fair Housing Act of 1968,[2] which was supposed to ban housing discrimination. Since these legislative actions and others designed to eradicate overt acts of racism, socioeconomic, educational, housing, health, and workplace outcomes have improved very little, if at all.

During The Winters Group's learning sessions, we sometimes engage participants in a "fact or fiction" exercise in which we display a statistic about some aspect of diversity and ask for a show of hands: "Is this fact or fiction?" A few of the race statistics that we sometimes include are the following. Test yourself before you look at the correct answers, shared in the next paragraph.

1. Black college graduates with similar backgrounds as whites have twice the unemployment rate.[3] *Fact/Fiction*
2. African American babies are twice as likely to die before their first birthday, regardless of the socioeconomic level of the mother.[4] *Fact/Fiction*
3. Blacks with advanced degrees earn about the same as their white counterparts with similar degrees.[5] *Fact/Fiction*

Do you think you got the right answers? Number 1 and number 2 are facts, and number 3 is fiction, because even after controlling for age, gender, education, and region, black workers with advanced degrees are paid 18.5 percent less than white workers. Were you surprised by any of these data? Many white participants in our sessions usually are. They say that they cannot believe that there are still such widespread disparities. Many of the people of color in the sessions are, however, not surprised.

While it is good to raise awareness, it is frustrating and fatiguing that session after session, white people are not aware that such inequities exist. In a recent conversation with a Black woman executive at a major health care organization, she lamented that it is "maddening" for her to sit in meetings with the CEO and his direct reports time and time again when they seem to be clueless about the structural racism that exists in their system. She said that even after years of training in cultural competence, antiracism, and unconscious bias, they do not seem to understand how the system perpetuates racism.

Stagnant Socioeconomic Progress

The most alarming and perhaps the most telling are the economic indicators. Black households have the lowest median household income and net worth of any demographic group, and those measures of progress have not improved. Unfortunately, then is now.

Figure 3.1 shows that Black household median income is the lowest of all groups and has only increased an infinitesimal amount ($62) in the last decade compared with much larger gains for whites and Hispanics.

Net worth is the difference between one's assets and liabilities. The net worth of white people was 10 times that of Black and Hispanic people in 2016 (figure 3.2).[6] While median net worth tends to increase for whites as levels of educational attainment rise, even controlling for educational differences the gap does not improve. For example, the median net worth of Black households headed by someone with at least a bachelor's degree was $26,300 in 2013, while for households headed by white college degree holders, the net worth was $301,300, 11 times that of Black people. In other words, contrary to logic, more education

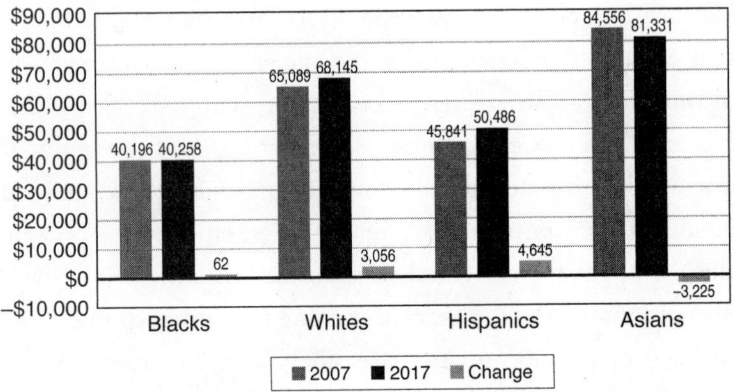

Figure 3.1. Change in median household income, 2007–2017
Source: The Winters Group based on data in Valerie Wilson, "10 Years after the Start of the Great Recession, Black and Asian Households Have Yet to Recover Lost Income."[7]

does not correlate with income equity. And shockingly, the median net worth of a single Black woman without a bachelor's degree is $500 and with a bachelor's degree is $5,000, while a single white woman has a median net worth of $8,000 without a bachelor's degree and $35,000 with one.[8]

A large part of this disparity is intergenerational wealth transfer. White people have the opportunity to transfer their assets to their children, giving them a head start with net worth. Generationally, Black families, because of the entrenched racist system, have not been able to amass wealth. As a matter of fact, many of us who have "good jobs" have to support our parents or other family members who have not been so fortunate, something known as the "Black tax." When you consider that nearly one in five Black families have zero or negative net worth, and Black household wealth is on track to reach zero by 2082,[9] it is hard to imagine the possibility of Blacks gaining financial freedom, let

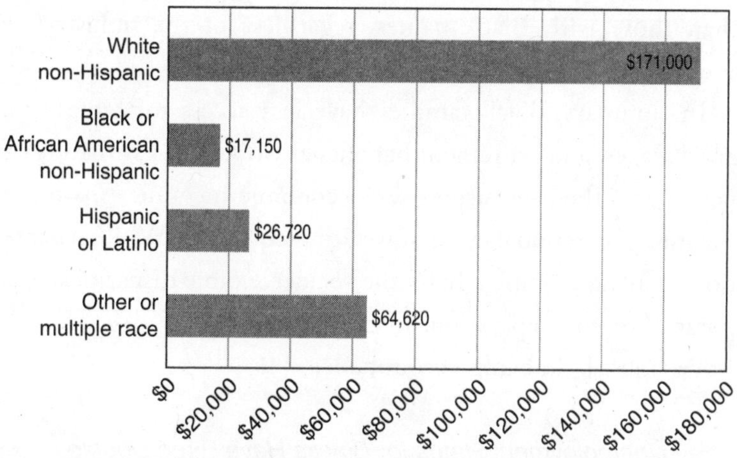

Figure 3.2. Median value of family net worth by race or ethnicity, 2016
Source: The Winters Group based on data in the Federal Reserve Board, "2016 Survey of Consumer Finances," 2017.

alone establishing generational wealth. Wealth is important to increase access to a better education, a healthy and safe living environment, better health care, and better job opportunities.

Several additional key factors exacerbate the vicious cycle of wealth inequality. Black households, for example, have far less access to tax-advantaged forms of savings, due in part to a long history of employment discrimination and lack of access to financial institutions. A well-documented history of mortgage market discrimination means that blacks are significantly less likely to be homeowners than whites and therefore are not able to access the tax advantages associated with home ownership, as discussed shortly. It is also well documented that Black people face more discrimination in the labor market and are more likely to be underpaid and underemployed. Studies show that applicants with white names are 50 percent more likely to get a callback than those with Black names, regardless of the industry or occupation.[10]

In summary, Black families have less access to stable jobs, good wages, and retirement benefits at work—all key drivers of net worth. These persistent socioeconomic inequities maintain the intergenerational cycle of wealth inequality.[11] While reparations may not completely fix the socioeconomic disparities, it is a start. I discuss reparations in chapter 9.

We must hold banks accountable.

Unemployment Rates for Blacks Have Been Double Those of Whites since the 1960s

Regardless of the time period, education level, or occupation, Black unemployment rates are twice those of whites, and this discrepancy has held steady since the 1960s (figure 3.3).[12] While

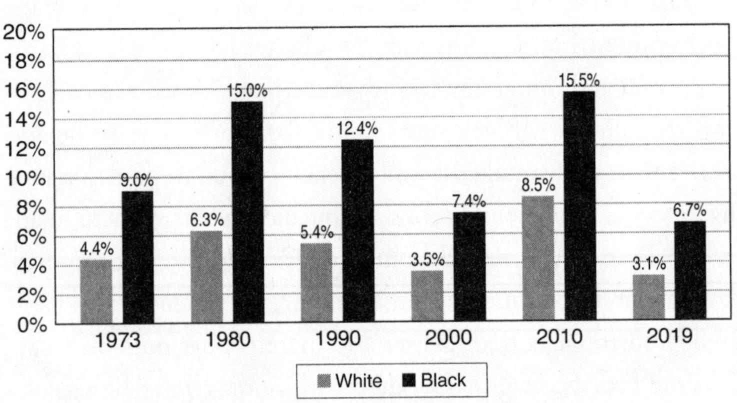

Figure 3.3. US unemployment rate by race, 1973–2019
Source: The Winters Group based on data in US Bureau of Labor Statistics, "Unemployment Rates by Sex, Race, and Hispanic or Latino Ethnicity."[13]

unemployment rates for every group were low in 2019 and have improved for marginalized groups, the disparity persists.

Home Ownership and Gentrification Continue to Stymie Progress

Black and Latino families are no more likely today to own their own home than they were in 1976, as shown in figure 3.4. Then is now.

Fifty years after the federal Fair Housing Act banned racial discrimination in mortgage lending, African Americans and Latinos continue to be regularly denied conventional mortgage loans at rates much higher than their white counterparts. In a study by the Center for Investigative Reporting in 2018 of 61 metropolitan areas, even when controlling for applicants' income, loan amount, and neighborhood, Black people were as much as 2.7 times less likely to be granted a loan.[14]

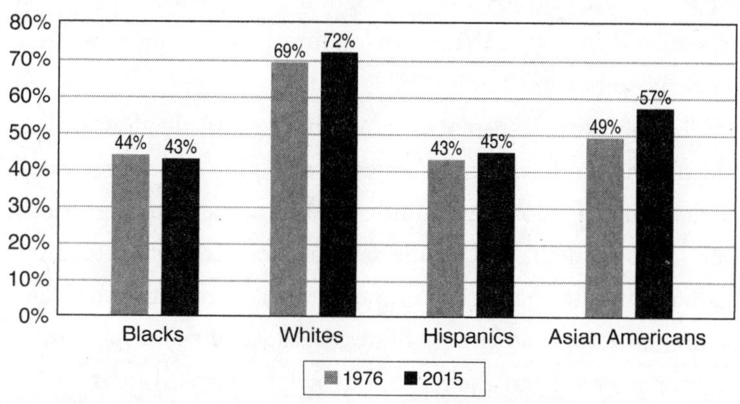

Figure 3.4. Home ownership
Note: The data for Asian Americans start in 1988.
Source: The Winters Group based on data in Pew Research Center, "Demographic Trends and Economic Well-Being."[15]

In the 1930s, surveyors with the federal Home Owners' Loan Corporation "legally" drew lines on maps all around the country, marking some neighborhoods red to indicate their rating as "hazardous" for bank lending because of the presence of African Americans or European immigrants, especially Jews. Under the Community Reinvestment Act of 1977,[16] banks had a legal obligation not only to not discriminate but also to solicit borrowers and depositors from all segments of their communities. This type of legislation has not quelled the systemic racism in housing. As a matter of fact, 75 percent of neighborhoods that had been marked "hazardous" in the Home Owners' Loan Corporation's redlined maps of the 1930s are still the most economically disadvantaged.[17] Then is now.

Relatedly, Blacks still largely live in segregated neighborhoods. According to the National Fair Housing Alliance, "In today's America, approximately half of all Black persons and 40 percent of all Latinos live in neighborhoods without a White presence. The average White person lives in a neighborhood that is nearly 80 percent White."[18]

Gentrification is also a key issue that negatively affects Black and Brown families. It is the systemic changing of underinvested, predominantly poor communities from low value to high value. Longtime residents and businesses are displaced, unable to afford higher rents, mortgages, and property taxes. Gentrification is happening all across the United States. Because of the displacement of poor people from their previous neighborhoods, it is almost impossible for them to find affordable housing. From Charlotte (where I live) to San Francisco (where I frequently consult), the lack of affordable housing is a problem of epic proportion.

In the 1960s gentrification was called "urban renewal" (a federally funded project to "clean up slums"). In a 1963 television interview, James Baldwin said, "Urban renewal is Negro removal."[19] Then is now.

The Workforce: Little Progress Has Been Made in Leadership Positions in the Workforce

Many companies continue to wrestle with the paucity of people of color in leadership ranks. Over three decades ago, when I started diversity and inclusion work, white male leaders lamented the lack of women and people of color in leadership roles and attributed it to their shorter tenure in large corporations (the Civil Rights Act of 1964 was only 20 years old). Today leaders still lament the lack of women and people of color in leadership roles, but the excuse now is that there are so few Black and Brown people with the qualifications that the competition is stiff, and they are lured away by other organizations. The reality is that Black people leave organizations because of the fatigue associated with needing to constantly prove themselves and not being acknowledged for their contributions, which I explore in later chapters.

Black employees with college or advanced degrees are also more likely than their white counterparts to be underemployed when it comes to their skill level. According to the Economic Policy Institute, 40 percent of Black workers are in jobs that do not typically require a college degree, compared with 31 percent of white college graduates.[20]

In the 1980s, a Black female friend of mine had risen through the ranks of a major corporation, but not until she had jumped through many more hurdles than her white male counterparts. She was a chemist by training and then got her MBA and then a doctorate in chemistry, as well as many professional certifications along the way. Tracy (not her real name) was always studying and working 70–80 hours per week. She was a director, trying to rise to vice president. Every time she asked what more she needed to do, there was another "something" that she needed. She retired from that organization and never made vice president. Tracy felt that she was micromanaged, required to be overeducated, and in the end undervalued and underappreciated. She retired early because she was burned out. Recent research by the Center for Talent Innovation reveals that these issues still continue to inhibit progress for Black women.[21] In healing sessions with Black employees during the Black Lives Matter movement protests of 2020, needing to be overqualified for consideration for promotions was a common theme. "You are never ready for the next level. No matter how many degrees or certifications you have, it is never enough." Then is now, and it is fatiguing.

Ascend, the largest nonprofit Pan-Asian organization for business professionals in North America,[22] developed the Executive Parity Index (EPI) to assess disparities in the leadership ranks. If the EPI is equal to 1.0, then a group's representation is the same at the top and bottom of the pipeline. If the EPI is less than 1.0, or below parity, then there are fewer at the top relative to those at the bottom. An EPI greater than 1.0 is above parity. Using the 2015 Equal Employment Opportunity Commission database of employment statistics by race, gender, and job classification and applying the formula, white men have an

EPI of 1.81; Hispanic men, 1.07; white women, 0.65; Black men, 0.63; Asian men, 0.56; Hispanic women, 0.49; Black women, 0.30; and Asian women, 0.24. Obviously, with the exception of Hispanic men, Black and Brown people are woefully below parity.[23]

This was a headline in 1984: "Many Blacks Jump Off the Corporate Ladder: Feeling Their Rise Limited" (*Wall Street Journal*, August 2, 1984). This was a headline in 2019: "Study Examines Why Black Americans Remain Scarce in Executive Suites" (*New York Times*, December 9, 2019). Then is now.

Several of my recent clients have initiated diversity efforts because their boards of directors are requiring it. These are the power brokers. Boards have the clout to dictate change. They are asking, Why are there so few people of color in leadership roles? Why do you have such a high turnover rate among people of color?

Most large organizations have a lot of work to do to change their cultures in order to move from rhetoric to sustained equity. I have personally been consulting on this for over three decades, and then is now.

Elected Officials

Of course, we all point to the pinnacle achievement in politics of the election of the first Black president, Barack Obama, in 2008 and again in 2012. While clearly a milestone, it did not come without backlash that we continue to contend with today. For many white people, Obama's election was proof positive that racism was no longer an issue in the United States—we could declare it a nasty, ugly thing of the past. It was deemed by many a sign of the advent of a postracial society. However, we started to see the backlash of his election very early on with death threats, personal attacks on his family, and a Congress that was determined to vote down any legislation that even remotely looked like it would benefit Black and Brown people. Many say that the election of Donald Trump was the ultimate backlash.

On a positive note, we have seen tremendous progress in increasing the representation of Black and Brown people in the House of Representatives; however, there has been little progress in the Senate. Fifty-two House members are Black, putting the share of Black House members (12 percent) on par with the share of Blacks in the US population overall for the first time in history.[24] Also, currently, 43 House members are Hispanic,[25] and 17 are Asian.[26]

The first Black US senator, Hiram R. Revels, a Republican from Mississippi, was chosen by his state's legislature to fill an empty seat. He served for a year, from 1870 to 1871. Since then, only nine other Black Americans have served in the Senate.

Voter Suppression

Then is now, in terms of voter suppression. The Thirteenth Amendment (1865) to the Constitution abolished slavery, the Fourteenth Amendment (1868) gave Black people equal rights, and the Fifteenth Amendment (1870) specifically prohibits the government from denying US citizens the right to vote based on race, color, or past servitude. The nation also adopted the Enforcement Acts between 1870 and 1871 that criminalized voter suppression and provided federal oversight in elections.[27] The Voting Rights Act of 1965 is considered landmark legislation to overcome legal barriers such as literacy tests and poll taxes that prevented African Americans from exercising their right to vote as guaranteed under the Fifteenth Amendment. The act called for federal oversight of voter registration in areas where less than 50 percent of the nonwhite population had registered to vote, and authorized the US attorney general to investigate the use of poll taxes in state and local elections.[28]

In 2013, the Supreme Court declared the oversight provision unconstitutional.[29] Striking down this requirement has increased voter suppression. In Georgia, Secretary of State Brian Kemp put over 50,000 voter registrations on hold, 70 percent of which were from Black residents. Several states with large and growing Black and Hispanic populations closed polling places: Texas closed over 400 polling places, Arizona closed over 200, and the states of Louisiana, Alabama, Mississippi, North Carolina, and South Carolina closed over 250.[30] These closures are a direct result of the Supreme Court's decision not to hold the Voting Rights Act intact.

In 2016, 6.1 million Americans, mostly people of color, were unable to vote because of a felony conviction.[31] Efforts to overturn such laws are often defeated. For example, voters in Florida passed legislation amending the state's constitution to restore voting rights to US citizens with prior felony convictions. This change would have meant that 1.4 million Floridians, including one in five Black residents, would regain their right to vote. However, Republican legislators in Tallahassee, led by Governor Ron DeSantis (R), circumvented this action by imposing new financial restrictions, such as fees unrelated to citizens' sentences, for people with prior felony convictions to vote.[32] These restrictions are similar to those of the Jim Crow era that perpetuated barriers to voting.

In 2018, the US Supreme Court's ruling in *Husted v. A. Philip Randolph Institute* increased the possibility for voter suppression in that states were permitted to eliminate eligible Americans from their voter rolls, also known as purging, if they decided to skip some elections.[33] The ruling supported Ohio's decision to purge 846,000 disproportionately Black voters from its rolls for infrequent voting over a six-year period.

In June 2019, the Supreme Court ruled that the federal government could not impede partisan gerrymandering on the state level, even though it admitted that gerrymandering could produce unfair outcomes.[34] New software maximizes partisan advantage, and since state legislatures are predominantly Republican, voting districts have been redrawn to the disadvantage of Democrats. Seventy-nine percent of Black people are registered Democrats, as are 62 percent of Latinos.[35]

Without political clout, it is impossible to change entrenched systems of discrimination. Too often, people of color are so fatigued from fighting these actions, they simply give up and do not vote, which leads to the increased chance of being purged from the rolls. Do you see how the system, not the people, is the problem?

Education

Public education is in crisis and has been for decades, with the most damaging impact on lower-income Black and Brown children.

The 1954 landmark *Brown v. Board of Education* Supreme Court decision banning segregation in public schools was the result of a hard-fought battle. Schools are more segregated today than in 1954. Children of color represent a majority of the student body in 83 of the 100 largest cities, and in all but three, at least half of them attend a school where a majority of their peers are poor or low income.[36] Researchers coined the term "apartheid schools" to describe schools where students of color form more than 99 percent of the population. Such schools educate one-third of the Black students in New York City and half of the Black students in Chicago. Nationwide, apartheid schools educate as many as 15 percent of Black students and 14 percent of Latinos.[37]

Studies also show that the more schools are integrated, the better Black students fare, including with lower dropout rates, higher standardized test scores, and improved outcomes for Blacks in areas such as earnings, health, and incarceration rates.[38] Racially diverse schools also benefit white students. Studies show that exposure to other students who are culturally and ethnically different from themselves leads to improved cognitive skills, including critical thinking and problem solving.[39]

Public schools attended by a majority of Black and Brown children are underfunded and underperforming. Despite decades of lawsuits throughout the country to eliminate the inequities, there remains a $23 billion gap in funding between school districts that serve predominantly Black and Brown students and those that serve white students, and they are serving the same number of students.[40] Between 2005 and 2017, US public schools were underfunded by $580 billion in Title 1 and Individuals with Disabilities Education Act federal dollars, money that is earmarked specifically to support 30 million of our most vulnerable students.[41]

The gap in standardized test scores of Black children appears before they enter kindergarten and persists into adulthood. While it has narrowed since 1970, on average Black children still score below 75 percent of American white students on almost every standardized test. The reasons for these differences are complex, and some experts say the gaps are more about teacher competencies and biases, lack of understanding of cultural differences, and how parents interact with their children than income, intelligence, or school funding.[42]

Research shows that non-Black teachers have lower expectations of Black students than Black teachers.[43] Black teachers only represent 10 percent of the teacher corps. Black men represent 2 percent of teachers. Black students are 3.8 times as likely as white students to receive one or more out-of-school suspensions.[44] While 6 percent of all K–12 students received one or more out-of-school suspensions, the percentage is 18 percent for Black boys, 10 percent for Black girls, 5 percent for white boys, and 2 percent for white girls. Black children represent 19 percent of the nation's preschool population, yet 47 percent of those receiving more than one out-of-school suspension. In comparison, white students represent 41 percent of preschool enrollment but only 28 percent of those receiving more than one out-of-school suspension. Black students are 2.3 times as likely as white students to receive a referral to law enforcement or get arrested because of a school-related problem.[45] These disparities are related to deeply entrenched biases that white teachers hold about the innocence and intelligence of Black children. I elaborate on this in chapter 8.

Even though there are a number of programs designed to recruit Black people into the teacher corps, many leave the profession after a few years because of the fatigue of not having the resources or support to do their job effectively. I remember some years ago the daughter of a friend of mine was required to make copies of textbook pages because there were not enough textbooks to go around. She paid for the copies from her first-year teacher's salary because the school did not have a copier that could handle the volume or a budget to cover the copies.

The problem is not the children. The problem is the system. The continued gross inequities in access to quality education for Black and Brown children and the rampant bias that leads to disproportionality in punishment are interconnected with life outcomes such as job opportunities and, ultimately, socioeconomic progress. And then there is legislation that disadvantages Black students. The current education secretary, Betsy DeVos, rescinded Obama-era legislation[46] on school discipline guidance that would have made it harder to suspend Black students. The policy was scrapped based on research the Trump administration relied on that showed that Black children are disciplined more than white children because Black children exhibit behavioral issues that start earlier in life, rather than because of institutional racism. The administration used this one data point and ignored mountains of other evidence to the contrary.[47] It is a vicious cycle that is fatiguing. Then is now.

Shifting the focus from the children as the problem to the system would lead us to:

- Lobby for policies that would provide equitable, not equal, funding to schools.
- Make teachers' salaries commensurate with their worth like those of valued professionals in a corporation.
- Focus on environmental racism in neighborhoods.
- Ensure that parents earn a living wage.
- Corporations should fund public education.

- Hold school administrators accountable for inequitable outcomes and refuse to accept rationale like parents are not involved and do not care about their children's education. Start with the premise that all parents care about their children's education and all children can learn. If they are not learning, there is something wrong with the system, not the children.

Criminal Justice

At the National Memorial for Peace and Justice in Montgomery, Alabama, more than 4,000 victims of racist lynching are remembered over the heads of visitors. From 1882 to 1968, 4,743 lynchings were recorded in the United States. Black people accounted for 72.7 percent of the people lynched. While these numbers seem large, the actual numbers are even bigger, because it is known that not all lynchings were recorded.[48]

While lynchings, as historically defined, may not be happening anymore, 26 percent of civilians killed by police shootings in 2015 were Black, even though Black civilians represent only 12 percent of the US population. And according to a study conducted in 2019 by Rutgers University's School of Criminal Justice, Washington University's Department of Sociology, and the University of Michigan's Institute for Social Research, in the United States African American men are 2.5 times more likely to be killed by police than white men. Black women are 1.4 times more likely than white women to be killed by police. The researchers used verified data from police records from 2013–2018.[49] Another study showed that 15 percent of the Black people police killed in 2015 were unarmed, compared with just 6 percent of white people who were unarmed when killed by police.[50]

A NewsOne story released in June reported that 83 Black men and boys have been killed by police since 2012.[51] In addition, in that same time frame, at least 22 Black women have been killed by law enforcement.

Police brutality had been going on long before 2009. As I mentioned in the preface, the Black Panther Party was started, in part, as a result of the killing of an unarmed Black 16-year-old in 1966. Protests erupted in Los Angeles in 1992 when three white policemen who had savagely beaten Rodney King a year earlier were acquitted.[52] In 1999, Amadou Diallo was fired on 41 times as he stood unarmed in the hallway of his apartment building. The officers involved in the case were acquitted.[53]

As many of these killings can be described as modern-day lynchings, in 2018 the House unanimously passed the Justice for Victims of Lynching Act, a law that criminalizes lynching for the first time in history. From 1882 to 1986 Congress failed to pass antilynching legislation 200 times.[54] The bill, introduced by Cory Booker (D-NJ), Kamala Harris (D-CA), and Tim Scott (R-SC), is stalled in the Senate as of this writing. Senator Rand Paul (R-KY) wants an amendment that would weaken the language in the bill.[55]

In 2017, Black people represented 12 percent of the total US population and 33 percent of the sentenced prison population. Whites accounted for 64 percent of the adult population and 30 percent of prisoners. And while Hispanics represented 16 percent of the adult population, they accounted for 23 percent of inmates. According to the Bureau of Justice Statistics, Native Americans are incarcerated at a rate 38 percent higher than the national average.[56] While the gap is narrowing between whites and Blacks in prison,[57] a Black boy born in 2001 still has a 1 in

3 chance of going to prison, while a white boy has a 1 in 17 chance.

Another gross inequity in the criminal justice system is that Black people represent a majority of innocent defendants wrongfully convicted of crimes and later exonerated. They constitute 47 percent of the 1,900 exonerations listed in the National Registry of Exonerations (as of October 2016) and the great majority of more than 1,800 additional innocent defendants who were framed and convicted of crimes in 15 large-scale police scandals and later cleared in "group exonerations."[58]

We must destigmatize Black people, men in particular, as criminals. The media plays a large role in this. Studies show that the media reports of murders, thefts, and assaults where Black people were suspects far outpaced their actual arrest rates for such crimes.[59] The media also portrays Black suspects as more threatening and scarier than whites by showing mug shots of Black suspects more frequently and perpetuating a narrative of white victimization.

Mass incarceration is a serious problem. The United States represents 5 percent of the world's population and has the highest incarceration rate in the world at 25 percent.[60] As chronicled in Michelle Alexander's landmark book *The New Jim Crow: Mass Incarceration in the Age of Colorblindness*,[61] from 1980 to 2000 the number of incarcerated people jumped from 300,000 to 2 million, with the majority of those being people of color. The impetus was President Ronald Reagan's War on Drugs program. Rather than categorizing drug abuse as a public health issue as it is today, largely because more white people are now addicted, the program labeled it as a crime and many people were sentenced to long jail terms without the possibility of parole.

Systemic racism continues even after release, with laws that disallow felons to vote or to find gainful employment. This leads to high recidivism rates.

SUMMARY

Then is now. Black people are fatigued because of the lack of progress in dismantling centuries-old racist systems. The forces that maintain the status quo are deeply entrenched. The widespread denial that racism is at the root of these interconnected issues is fatiguing and literally killing those who are the victims of this system.

We must first change the narrative. Current strategies, by and large, focus on Black people as the problem rather than intractable racist systems. We put Band-Aids on the issues with programs primarily designed to fix Black people. If corporations want to help, they will not only offer passive support by declaring Juneteenth a holiday and increasing their philanthropic dollars earmarked for Black-serving institutions, they will become actively engaged in lobbying for antiracist legislation. They will no longer be nonpartisan. They will dedicate resources to understanding and addressing both external and internal racism from the roots up.

Of all the forms of inequality, injustice in health is the most shocking and inhuman.

—Martin Luther King Jr., scholar, minister, and leader of the American civil rights movement

FOUR

Racism Literally Makes You Sick: It Is a Preexisting Condition

Fannie Lou Hamer, a Black civil rights activist, said in 1964, "I am sick and tired of being sick and tired."[1] She was referring to the fatigue associated with fighting for rights that were supposedly guaranteed by the Constitution. This is now an iconic refrain that many Black and Brown people understand at their core and repeat to each other with no other words necessary because there is a collective understanding of exactly what it means. Racism exhausts Black people. We live in a world that for centuries has dehumanized, ostracized, murdered, and otherwise violated our human rights. The intergenerational fatigue that comes from enduring structural racism literally makes you sick.

This chapter is for both Black and white readers. I must admit that I was not in tune with the impact of racism on my physical and mental health until recently. The millennials on my team started to talk about rest as a form of resilience, the Nap

Ministry,[2] and self-care. I felt confident that I took care of myself. I exercise, follow nutrition guidelines, and get eight hours of sleep most nights. However, as someone who does diversity, equity, inclusion, and justice work for a living and lives while Black, I had to do some serious self-reflection on whether I was really attending to my well-being. And while I initially pooh-poohed the millennials' focus on the extra self-care Black people may need, I came to understand the merit in their wisdom. At the height of the 2020 Black Lives Matter protests, I experienced palpable pain, stress, and rage and witnessed the same in some of my colleagues. There was crying and hyperventilating, and a few acknowledged they were on the brink of a meltdown. While these were unusually stressful times because those of us in the work were being bombarded with requests for urgent healing and listening sessions to quell the tensions and being in the middle of COVID-19, I now acknowledge the low-level, ongoing stress that I described at the beginning of chapter 1, "My Black Fatigue."

As Black people, we need to pay attention to our health.

Racism Leads to Health Disparities

There is a common saying in the Black community that when the world gets a cold, Black people get pneumonia, and when the world gets pneumonia, Black people die. The recent coronavirus pandemic put a spotlight on this unfortunate reality. In many communities, Black people died at two to four times their representation in the population.[3] This chapter details the glaring health disparities between Black and white people and their causes.

According to Families USA, a national, nonpartisan voice for health care consumers, in 2019, these major health disparities existed between Black and white people:[4]

- Black people are 44 percent more likely to die from a stroke.
- Black people are 20 percent more likely to have asthma and three times more likely than white people to die from it.
- Black people are 25 percent more likely to die from heart disease.
- Black women are 40 percent more likely to die from breast cancer.
- Black women are 52 percent more likely to die from cervical cancer and 40 percent more likely to die from breast cancer than white women, even though the incident rate of breast cancer is comparable for the two groups.[5]
- Black women are 243 percent more likely than white women to die from pregnancy- or child-birth-related causes.[6] College-educated Black women have worse birth outcomes (e.g., infant mortality, low birth weights, dying in childbirth) than white women who have not finished high school.
- Black women represent more than 66 percent of new HIV/AIDS cases.
- Black men are 30 percent more likely and Black women 60 percent more likely to be diagnosed with high blood pressure.
- Black men are 1.3 times more likely to be diagnosed with colon cancer and 20 percent more likely to die from it.
- Black people are 20 percent more likely to report psychological distress.

- Black infants are 3.5 times more likely to die at birth because of low birth weight.
- Black infants have 2.2 times higher infant mortality rates, regardless of the socioeconomic status of the mother.
- Black children are twice as likely to die from sudden infant death syndrome.
- Black children are twice as likely to have asthma.
- Black children are 56 percent more likely to be obese.
- Black children are 61 percent more likely to attempt suicide as high schoolers as a result of depression.

Health disparities result in lower life expectancies for Black people than any other ethnic group. According to data from the Centers for Disease Control and Prevention,[7] in 2017, the life expectancy in the United States for all races was 78.6 years and the lowest for African Americans at 75.3 years—even lower for African American men at 71.9 years, compared with the life expectancy for whites at 78.8 years.[8] Figure 4.1 compares white, African American, and Hispanic life expectancy.[9] The life expectancy for Black men has declined since 2011, when it was 72.2 years.

Researchers have coined a term—"excess deaths"—to explain the difference in life expectancy. If Blacks and whites had the same mortality rate, nearly 100,000 fewer Black people would die each year in the United States. Even educated Black people are sicker and die younger than their educated white peers. A Black person will live, on average, about three fewer years than a white person with the same income.[10]

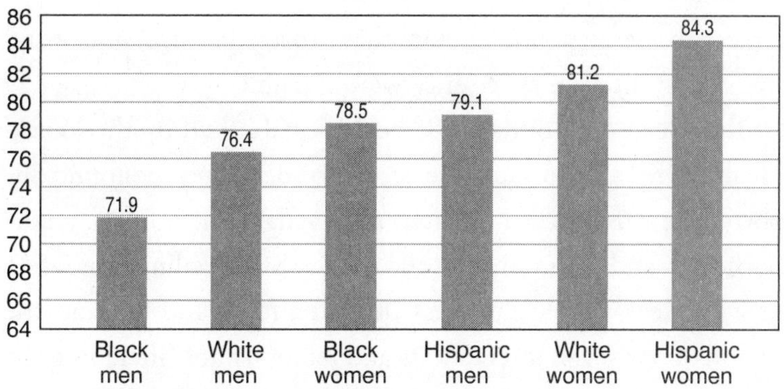

Figure 4.1. Life expectancy by race and sex, 2017
Source: The Winters Group based on data in "USA Life Expectancy," USA Health Rankings.[11]

Racism Causes Chronic Stress

There is a plethora of research to support the health disadvantage related to the harmful effects of chronic experiences with race-based discrimination, both real and perceived. These stressful experiences are thought to set into motion a process of physiological responses (e.g., elevated blood pressure and heart rate, production of biochemical reactions, hypervigilance) that eventually result in disease and mortality.[12] For example, researchers found that factors that predispose individuals to negative mental health outcomes include unfair treatment and social disadvantage, as well as other social stressors, such as inadequate levels of social support, and the occurrence of everyday life events. Other studies examined the possible consequences of perceived discrimination and found that just the anticipation of being treated badly or unfairly had as powerful an impact on individuals' mental and physical states. Medical experts report that being socially rejected, experiencing stereotypes, and suffering discrimination trigger the same neural circuits that process physical injury and translate it into the experience we call pain.[13]

The social determinants of health established by the World Health Organization include access to social and economic opportunities; resources and supports available in homes, neighborhoods, and communities; the quality of schooling; the safety of workplaces; the cleanliness of water, food, and air; and the nature of our social interactions and relationships (including the effects of racism).[14] For a disproportionate number of Black and Brown people, these basic requirements for good health are absent because of structural racism, contributing to greater stress and more fatigue in pursuit of them.

Auburn University released the results of a study in February 2020 that concluded that African Americans who reported more experiences with racial discrimination aged faster,[15] adding to the evidence that racism is not only a "social and moral dilemma" but also a public health issue. Nearly 400 African Americans from Birmingham, Chicago, Minneapolis, and Oakland, California, participated in the study, which began in 2000, and the participants, on average, were 40 years old at the study's inception. According to the results, encountering racism led to higher levels of stress, which in turn caused cells to age more rapidly. This study focused on its effects on telomeres, pieces of DNA that protect cells. The study proves that a particular type of social toxin that disproportionately affects African Americans becomes embedded at the cellular level.

Another study, conducted in 2019 by Georgia State University, corroborates the findings of the Auburn University study. This study found that experiencing discrimination early in life led to chronic worrying about it, which can cause significant "wear and tear" by increasing one's allostatic load, the lifelong buildup of stress, which accelerates aging and puts African Americans at greater risk for chronic illnesses.[16]

In summary, racism contributes to Black people's getting sick at younger ages and having more severe illnesses, which leads to more rapid aging. Scientists call this the "weathering hypothesis," or the result of cumulative stress.

While we might think that higher socioeconomic status mitigates these outcomes, according to a study done by Ohio State University researchers, the self-reported health status got worse for Black people as they climbed the socioeconomic ladder as opposed to whites, who reported better health based on higher socioeconomic status.[17] The pressure of navigating a white power structure to maintain your status can be daunting. Middle-class, educated Black people may fare worse in health because they are exposed to increased opportunities for discrimination, some of it subtle and in the form of microaggressions discussed in chapter 6, that multiply and increase stress. There may also be a higher chance for tokenism as upwardly mobile Black and Brown people find themselves as the only one or one of a few who have risen to their status in the organization. The pressure, real or perceived, that we represent the race adds to the level of stress. Even with all the rhetoric that we are individuals and do not represent or speak for the entire race, the reality is that often we feel we do. During healing sessions we conducted for several clients at the height of the Black Lives Matter protests in 2020, we consistently heard the following from Black employees about their experience in corporate America:

- There is no room for mistakes.
- We have to justify our reason for being.
- I am forever standing on a soapbox screaming for equality.
- I am on the defensive all of the time.
- I am stressed to the max trying to fit in and be myself at the same time.
- Black people run from the narrative of being lazy so we overwork ourselves, fearing that stereotype.
- I am isolated, alone, and misunderstood.
- We have to speak for all Black people.
- Whether we like it or not, we represent the race.

The extra emotional toll that it requires to succeed in corporate America is stressful and can affect one's physiological and psychological health.

Place-Based Fear Exacerbates Stress

Race-based health effects are often unrecognized and therefore are an unacknowledged phenomenon. There are many aspects of living while Black that can induce negative health consequences. The most serious source of this is fear for our lives. It is stress inducing to worry about your safety and that of your loved ones.

We can look throughout history at many situations in which Black people have been killed for being in the wrong place, allegedly doing the wrong thing. I mentioned the numerous lynchings throughout history in chapter 3 and Emmett Till in the preface. As mentioned in the last chapter, there are a number of high-profile cases in recent history, such as those of Trayvon Martin (2012), Michael Brown (2014), Tamir Rice (2014),

Botham Jean (2019), Philando Castile (2016), Eric Garner (2014), and the most recent ones that sparked the 2020 Black Lives Matter protests—Ahmaud Arbery (2020), Breonna Taylor (2020), and George Floyd (2020). Less publicized cases of Black women being killed by police include those of Shelly Frey (2102), Eleanor Bumpurs (1984), Margaret Laverne Mitchell (1999), and Sandra Bland (2015), among others. These incidents are devastating for the families and for other Black people who empathize with the victims of brutality and hold the fear that it could have been them or someone close to them. Compounding the devastation is the fact that in most cases there is no justice. The police officers who perpetrate these heinous crimes are most often acquitted based on self-defense or stand-your-ground claims. Between 2005 and April 2017, 80 officers had been arrested on murder or manslaughter charges for on-duty shootings. During that 12-year span, 35 percent were convicted, while the rest were pending or not convicted, according to work by Philip Stinson, an associate professor of criminal justice at Bowling Green State University in Ohio.[18]

There can be a great deal of anxiety associated with daily concerns about how the color of your skin will affect even the simplest interactions. I call this "place-based" fear—when you find yourself in a place where you might not be welcome. It is common for Black people to ask, Is it OK to go to that part of town? Is it OK to visit that country? How do they treat Black people there? There is a fear of being in a place where you will experience racial profiling and the dire consequences that might result.

While a student at Harvard, my son, Joe, and some friends (all Black) were studying late at night in an on-campus lounge.

Apparently, someone called security and they were questioned about their right to be there, doubting that they could possibly be Harvard students. While maybe not a life-threatening fear, I am sure that these young men experienced some level of anxiety as to what might happen to them.

Right around that same time in 2018, three Black people were checking out of a California Airbnb when seven police cars arrived and demanded that they put their hands in the air; a neighbor had reported a robbery in progress because she saw them loading luggage into a car. The ordeal took 45 minutes to resolve and included a helicopter being summoned and the need to show proof that they had rented the house. One of the three, a filmmaker, chronicled the ordeal on Facebook. "We have been dealing with different emotions and you want to laugh about this but it's not funny," she wrote. "The trauma is real. I've been angry, frustrated and sad. I was later detained at the airport. This is insanity."[19]

Place-based stress manifests even with seemingly innocuous daily events like shopping. Black people are targeted and followed in department stores more often and profiled as thieves. There may also be assumptions about their ability to pay. Oprah encountered this situation in a Swiss department store several years ago where she was considering purchasing a very expensive purse ($38,000!) and the salesperson did not recognize her and refused to let her see it because it was too expensive.[20] I had this happen numerous times when I was trying to purchase items—not anywhere close to Oprah's league, mind you, but apparently to the salesperson I looked like I could not afford them. These situations affected how I approached salespeople. When they were younger, my kids would ask me why I was so mean when I entered a department store. I would say, "What are you talking about? I am not mean." I realized that because I had been treated so poorly in past situations, I had my defenses up. Unconsciously, I was thinking, "Nobody is going to mistreat me today." These race-based experiences elicit not only fear but also frustration and even anger, inciting the "angry Black woman" stereotype and adding stress.

Even scarier is being in the wrong place at the wrong time and facing the threat of being misidentified. In 2018 a 21-year-old Black man was killed by a police officer who thought he was involved in a melee in a mall. They very soon afterward realized that he was not the shooter[21] and in fact was trying to deescalate the situation. In February 2020, I was in the Moline, Illinois, airport working on this book when I started to listen to a news report about a Black young man who attended Eastern Illinois University. Illinois police officers wrongfully arrested, detained, and threatened to shoot 19-year-old Jaylan Butler while pointing a gun to his forehead at a rest stop as he traveled with the school's swim team.[22] These are just two examples of many situations that I hear about on an almost daily basis that engender fear, increasing the stress of living while Black.

Constantly living with the perceived or real threats associated with the color of our skin leads to greater internalized stress, which in turn leads to physiological and psychological illnesses that disproportionately affect us.

Unfortunately, many may not associate their physical and emotional symptoms with race-based stress, which can manifest as the more serious condition of trauma.

Racism Leads to Race-Based Intergenerational Trauma

Race-based trauma has been getting more attention over the past decade. Robert Carter, professor of psychology and education in the Department of Counseling and Clinical Psychology at Teachers College, Columbia University, is an expert in what he has termed race-based traumatic stress injury, defined as the emotional and psychological trauma caused by discrimination and racism that elicit responses comparable to those associated with posttraumatic stress injury. One may express the trauma through anxiety, anger, rage, depression, low self-esteem, or shame, and it may manifest as depression, fatigue, diseases such as high blood pressure or diabetes, or mental disorders.[23]

Author and former college professor in social work Joy DeGruy coins the term "posttraumatic slave syndrome" in a book by the same name, defining it as "a condition that exists when a population has experienced multigenerational trauma resulting from centuries of slavery and continues to experience oppression and institutionalized racism today. Adding to this condition is a belief (real or imagined) that the benefits of the society in which they live are not accessible to them."[24] She asserts that survivor syndrome manifests in the second and third generations as stress, self-doubt, problems with aggression, and a number of psychological and interpersonal relationship problems with family members and others.

Social scientists have also coined the term "historical trauma"[25] to refer to the multigenerational, communal trauma that oppressed and marginalized groups have faced. In a 2013 article in the *Atlantic* called "How Racism Is Bad for Our Bodies," the author points out that the cyclical effects of discrimination lead to "embodied inequality," which creates poor health outcomes that are passed down from generation to generation. The result is a vicious cycle in which the sickest and poorest remain sick and poor.[26] The cycle starts with young children, which I discuss in chapter 8.

A growing and somewhat controversial branch of science, epigenetics, studies the extent to which our social environments can alter gene activity that can be passed down from generation to generation. Shannon Sullivan, chair and professor of philosophy at the University of North Carolina at Charlotte, penned an article, "Inheriting Racist Disparities in Health: Epigenetics and the Transgenerational Effects of White Racism," which outlines how people of color can biologically inherit the harmful effects of racism. She uses preterm birth rates as an example. Black women (16.8 percent), regardless of income, are more likely than other groups (10.3 percent for white women) to deliver early, and this has been connected to accumulated stress. This disparity has not improved since the 1970s.[27]

Implicit and Explicit Bias Contribute to Lower-Quality Health Care

In 2003, the Institute of Medicine, now called the National Academy of Medicine, released a landmark report called *Unequal Treatment*, which outlined stark health disparities for nonwhite populations. Among the findings were that poverty, lack of insurance, or lack of access did not totally account for the fact that Black people are sicker and have shorter life-spans than white people. The study found that "racial and ethnic minorities receive lower-quality health care than white people—even when insurance status, income, age, and severity of conditions are comparable." The National Academy of Medicine reported that people of color were less likely than white people to be given appropriate cardiac care, to receive kidney dialysis or transplants, and to receive the best treatments for strokes, cancer, or AIDS. Its conclusion: "Some people in the United States were more likely to die from cancer, heart disease, and diabetes simply because of their race or ethnicity, not just because they lack access to health care." This study shed light on the stark reality that race is a determinant of the quality of health care in this country.[28]

Sadly, not much has changed in health outcomes for Black and Brown people in the almost 20 years since that report was released. A number of newer studies show that Black and Brown people continue to have disparate health outcomes, as presented at the beginning of this chapter, and continue to be subjected to the racial biases, conscious or implicit, of health care providers. Here are a few examples:

- According to an October 2015 report in *JAMA Internal Medicine*, published by the American Medical Association, on average, white Americans spent 80 minutes waiting for or receiving care, while Black Americans spent 99 minutes and Latinos 105 minutes waiting for or receiving that same care.[29]
- Black and Hispanic patients in US emergency rooms are less likely to receive medication to ease acute pain than their

white counterparts. Researchers examined data from 14 previously published studies in American emergency rooms that included 7,070 white patients, 1,538 Hispanic patients, and 3,125 Black patients. The study found that compared with white patients, Black patients were 40 percent less likely to receive medication to ease acute pain and Hispanic patients were 25 percent less likely. The study's authors concluded that while the reasons are complex, unconscious bias was likely a contributing factor.[30]

- A study of 400 hospitals in the United States showed that Black patients with heart disease received older, cheaper, and more conservative treatments than their white counterparts. Black patients were less likely to receive coronary bypass operations and angiography. After surgery, they are discharged earlier from the hospital than white patients—at a stage when discharge is inappropriate.[31]
- Black women are less likely than white women to receive mastectomies in general and radiation therapy in conjunction with a mastectomy.[32]
- Black people are less likely to be prescribed newer medicine for mental disorders. Rather, they tend to be offered older medicine with worse side effects. Specifically, a drug called clozapine, which is considered to be superior psychiatric medicine, is prescribed less in minority patients with serious mental illness when compared with white patients.[33]
- Middle-class black women are still three to four times more likely to die in childbirth than white women. Lack of access to quality medical care and other social factors being ruled out, experts say racism, not race, is the cause.[34]

Evidence that implicit bias, defined as unconscious attitudes or stereotypes about a particular social group that influence behaviors, contributes to these disparities comes from results of administering the Implicit Association Test to physicians. The Implicit Association Test,[35] developed by Harvard researchers, measures the strength of associations between race and evaluations (e.g., good or bad). One study showed that physicians with Implicit Association Test scores that revealed them to have pro-white implicit biases were more likely to prescribe pain medications to white patients than to black patients. In another study, physicians with pro-white biases were less likely to prescribe thrombolysis to black patients and more likely to prescribe the treatment to white patients.

Environmental Racism Disproportionately Impacts Black Communities

One of the social determinants of health is where you live, and many poor Black and Brown people live in what are called "food deserts." Studies show that poverty and race both matter in having access to healthy food options. When comparing communities, research shows that Black and Hispanic neighborhoods have fewer large supermarkets and more small grocery stores than their white counterparts with similar poverty levels.[36] Many major grocery chains and restaurants choose not to locate in Black neighborhoods. Persistent redlining and economic inequality, as mentioned in chapter 3, limit opportunities for where many Black people can live. Many of the neighborhoods are packed with unhealthy fast-food restaurants and small convenience stores (with higher prices), which leads to high rates of childhood obesity and other chronic conditions such as high blood pressure and heart disease.

Not only are many of these neighborhoods food deserts, they also have poor-quality drinking water, high levels of lead, and fewer green spaces, all contributing to poorer health outcomes. The Environmental Protection Agency's National Center for Environmental Assessment released a study in 2018 indicating that people of color are much more likely to live near polluters and breathe polluted air. The study found that Black people are exposed to about 1.5 times more pollutants than white people, and that Hispanics had about 1.2 times the exposure of non-Hispanic whites.[37]

These findings were against a backdrop of the Environmental Protection Agency's and the Trump administration's plans to dismantle many of the institutions built to address those disproportionate risks.

Access to Quality Care is Still an Issue

While the disparities in access to mental and physical health care have improved greatly over the years, they persist. The Affordable Care Act improved access to care. According to a study by the Commonwealth Fund, between 2013 and 2015, disparities narrowed for Blacks and Hispanics on three key access indicators: the percentage of uninsured working-age adults, the percentage who did not seek care because of costs, and the percentage who did not have a primary care provider.[38]

Under the Affordable Care Act, uninsured rates for Blacks decreased from 19 percent to 10.7 percent from 2013 to 2017 and from 30 percent to 19 percent for Latinos and from 12 percent for

7 percent for whites for the same time period. However, these gains started to show statistically significant declines under the Trump administration. The Trump administration has made several changes to the act's implementation, altering the availability of coverage and the likelihood that people would enroll. As a result, both whites and Blacks had small but statistically significant increases in their uninsured rates in 2017, which rose by 0.2 percentage points for whites, from 7.1 percent to 7.3 percent, and by 0.4 percentage points for Blacks, from 10.7 percent to 11.1 percent. These types of changing policies, which are at the whim of changing political ideologies, add to the fatigue of not being assured that gains will be sustained.[39]

Compounding the access issue is the fact that studies show, for example, that people of color are less likely to seek mental health solutions, even when accessible, as there is a cultural stigma attached. In the African American and Latino communities, many people misunderstand what a mental health condition is and don't talk about this topic.[40] This lack of knowledge leads many to believe that a mental health condition is a personal weakness. According to a study by Cigna,[41] Black people are 50 percent less likely to receive counseling or mental health treatment.

Black People Are More Likely to Distrust Medical Professionals

Complicating the access issue is trust. In a 2007 study reported in the *American Journal of Public Health*, Blacks and Hispanics reported higher levels of physician distrust than did whites. In general, lower socioeconomic status (defined as lower income, lower education, and no health insurance) was associated with higher levels of distrust, and men reported more distrust than women.[42]

There is a long history of discrimination against and exploitation of Black Americans and other marginalized groups in the health system, which contributes to continued mistrust. The intergenerational memory of medicine's using Black people for experimentation without our consent is deeply embedded in our collective consciousness. In the antebellum period, Blacks were forced to serve as subjects for dissections, and corpses robbed from graves served as a constant source of surgical experimentation. The psychiatric definition of "drapetomania" ("runaway slave syndrome") was created as a "diagnosis" for African slaves who fled their slave masters. The treatment was often amputation of extremities.

During Reconstruction, white doctors advanced a theory that former slaves would not thrive in a free society because, psychologically, their minds could not handle freedom. In the civil rights era, psychiatrists called civil rights activists schizophrenic and labeled them as violent, hostile, and paranoid, which is one reason why Black people have an aversion to acknowledging mental health concerns.

The Tuskegee syphilis study, in which hundreds of Black men, without their consent, were intentionally administered syphilis and denied treatment, became the very embodiment of the way medicine and medical research was used against Black Americans. The Tuskegee experiments are a prime example of why the Black community distrusts physicians and research. Just this year, a French scientist recommended using African people as human guinea pigs to test a vaccine for the coronavirus. The doctor later apologized and said that his comments were misinterpreted.[43]

Henrietta Lacks was a Black woman who died in 1951 at age 31 of cervical cancer. Without her family's knowledge or consent, her cancer cells, which carried a unique replication quality, were shared with researchers for decades. Known as the HeLa cell line, Henrietta's contribution aided the development of the Salk polio vaccine and enhanced understanding of bacterial infection, HIV, and tuberculosis, among other diseases. Her cells revolutionized the field of medicine, and it was not until 2010, when a book was published entitled *The Immortal Life of Henrietta Lacks*,[44] that this story became known. In 2013 her family reached an agreement with the National Institutes of Health to allow continued use of the cells and to acknowledge Lacks's contribution. The agreement, however, did not provide any financial compensation.

Harriet A. Washington forcefully argues in her book *Medical Apartheid: The Dark History of Medical Experimentation on Black Americans from Colonial Times to Present* that racial discrimination has shaped both the relationship between white physicians and Black patients and the attitudes of Black people toward modern medicine in general. She speaks to the cultural memory of medical experimentation and the complex relationship between racism and medicine.[45]

This intergenerational lack of trust caused by the unethical practices of the medical profession targeted at Black people often keeps us from seeking care, exacerbating the disparities.

What Are the Solutions?

The complexities of racial inequities inherent in the health care and associated systems make it very difficult and too often impossible for Black people to sustain healthy minds, bodies and spirits. The problems are intergenerational, interconnected multidimensional and need to be addressed inside and outside the health care system.

Systems-Level Solutions

While there are no easy fixes, continuing to raise awareness helps tremendously. We must continue to fund the academic research that is bringing these inequities to light and ensure that cultural competence and implicit bias training is included in curricula for health care professionals. While studies show that over the last 20 years more medical schools are including cultural competence training in their programs, it is still inconsistent in application and content, and experts admit improvements are needed.[46]

More policies need to be enacted to establish strategies to minimize racism in the health care system. As an example, in 2019, the American Association of Pediatrics issued its first policy on racism's impact on child health. It establishes practical strategies to mitigate racism at the structural, interpersonal, and intrapersonal levels. Among other things, it calls for trauma-informed care.[47] Such care reframes the thinking of the caregiver from "What is wrong with this person?" to "What has happened to this person?"

Recognizing that health care professionals do not always receive adequate training in cultural competence, The Winters Group developed a comprehensive training program for large hospital systems, called "Radical Inclusion." A three-day immersion experience, it is designed to support leaders, physicians, and other medical professionals in enhancing the patient experience. We chose the term "radical" because of its meaning—"relating to or affecting the fundamental nature of something; far-reaching or thorough." Inclusion incorporates the tenets of cultural competence—the ability to discern, respect, and consider cultural differences in decision-making, problem solving, and conflict resolution. We want participants to think about the needed change as not incremental but transformational. The learning experience focuses on developing cultural self-understanding, understanding cultural differences, building alliances across differences, and engaging in bold, inclusive conversations.

Intrapersonal and Interpersonal Solutions

It is important to address the physiological and psychological toll at the individual level. We often internalize racism, unconsciously or consciously embodying negative stereotypes that white supremacist culture has about Black people. In our interpersonal relationships, we are regularly subjected to racist verbal attacks or worse, heightening stress and anxiety. We have learned a multitude of ways to take care of our mental and physical health.

Ardent Belief in God Black people, as a group, are strong in their Christian faith. According to a Pew survey, 75 percent of Blacks versus 49 percent of whites say that religion is very important to them,[48] and 54 percent of Black people—both Christian and non-Christian—say they read the Bible at least once a week outside of religious services, compared with 32 percent of whites.[49] Even though slaves did not come to the United States as Christians, they soon embraced the religion's tenets. After the Civil War, the Black church movement grew quickly, and it continues to play a key role in strengthening Black communities by providing spiritual as well as socioeconomic support.

Black people rely on our belief in God as a primary way of enduring the pain of racism. From the days of slavery, believing that God would see us through kept us from giving up. During Black History Month, especially, songs like "We've Come This Far by Faith" and the Negro National Anthem, "Lift Every Voice and Sing"—"Sing a song full of the faith that the dark past has taught us, / sing a song full of the hope that the present has brought us; / facing the rising sun of our new day begun, / let us march on till victory is won"—are commonly sung. Preacher and politician Adam Clayton Powell's famous refrain, "Keep the faith," sums up what many Black people do to survive and thrive in a racist world. Disconnecting from the temporal and operating at a higher level of consciousness that transcends our earthly existence is how we often find joy and peace.

Self-Care Self-care is critical for everyone who faces the stresses associated with racism and other isms. Black and Brown people are learning to lean on strategies such as mindfulness to heal the intergenerational fatigue of racism. In her book *The Inner Work of Racial Justice: Healing Ourselves and Transforming Our Communities through Mindfulness*, lawyer and mindfulness practitioner Rhonda Magee provides practical strategies for individuals "to process the pain that arises when we push ourselves or are pushed by others outside of our racial-identity comfort zone."[50] She says the practice of mindfulness can help us in knowing ourselves, becoming more familiar with the habits of our minds and our own emotional reactions of anger, confusion, numbness, and outrage when we see racism. It helps us to become more self-compassionate, she asserts, minimizing the impact of encountering racism. Practices such as meditation, yoga, journaling, and reflection, when done with intention and consistency, can be helpful.

In partnership with My True Self, a socially conscious wellness coaching and consulting practice, The Winters Group launched the Physiology of Inclusion in particular to support people in managing the emotional toll associated with diversity, equity, and inclusion (DEI) work. It is a whole-body system to raise awareness and enable strategies for resilience that improve physical, mental, and emotional health specifically targeted to DEI practitioners. However, this system can support anyone in a marginalized group. This system comprises the three foundational elements of eating, sleeping, and exercising that precede the three enabling elements necessary for enacting inclusion: thinking, being, and interacting. Too often we hear about the emotional, mental, and physical toll DEI can take on a person's health and ability to stay engaged in the work. It is important to prioritize our well-being if we are truly going to be effective in shifting organizational cultures and influencing systems. Through the partnership with My True Self, The Winters Group offers coaching and virtual and in-person learning experiences.

At the interpersonal level, healing circles have become a popular approach for groups to come together to share individual truths, history, and stories. Based on Indigenous and African traditions, healing circles affirm and validate Black voices. The circle is set up so that each person has an opportunity to share his or her story or truth without judgment and uninterrupted. Borrowing from Native American practices, sometimes a talking stick is passed around and only the person with the talking stick is allowed to speak. With the guidance of a skilled facilitator, the desired outcome is to support each person in the group in his or her healing journey.

As one example, Safe Black Space Community Healing Circles[51] were launched in 2018 in response to increased racial tension and trauma in the Sacramento, California, community after the killing by police of Stephon Clark, an unarmed Black man. The monthly Safe Black Space Healing Circles are for people who self-identify as being of African ancestry and are experiencing racial, stress, anxiety, or trauma. Sessions include African-centered healing strategies such as libations and drumming, mindfulness, and other self-care exercises. There are many other organizations that sponsor healing circles throughout the country.

Healing and Resilience Are Not Cures Healing and resilience techniques are important for staying physically and mentally well. However, such approaches deal with the symptoms and do not fix the underlying systems that cause the need to heal. "Resilience" connotes bouncing back from difficult experiences. If the difficult experiences never go away, the situation begins to bear a resemblance to that of Sisyphus in Greek mythology. His boulder started rolling down the hill right when he thought he was nearing the top. Why are Black and Brown people still required to push boulders up hills anyway? In a post in The Winters Group's *Inclusion Solution* blog, Thamara Subramanian, learning and innovation manager at our firm, eloquently points out that "the rise of resilience training in corporate settings has been misconstrued as a sustainable solution to wellness—ultimately putting the burden of problems driven by the organization onto the individual. This is essentially a company saying to its employees: *'Hey, the discrimination and adversities you face here at work will lessen if you gain the tools to bounce back . . . [because] the -isms you face . . . are just a part of life.'*"[52]

Reframing Our Own Narrative Positive self-talk that transforms into positive attitudes and behaviors can be helpful (figure 4.2).

FROM:	TO:
Being Black is exhausting.	Racism is exhausting.
Black people are more prone to certain diseases. It is inevitable.	Systemic racism affects my health. I need to understand the influence of white supremacy on my well-being and not internalize it.
I do not have time for self-care.	There is at least one thing I can do for me every day to lessen the stress of living while Black.
I do not go to doctors because I do not trust them.	I will seek out a Black doctor whom I might feel more comfortable with.
The doctor said I have . . .	Question the results. Question the recommended treatment options. Get a second and third opinion. Do your own research.

Figure 4.2. Narrative reframing
Source: The Winters Group.

SUMMARY

Racism is a significant factor contributing to health disparities that affect Black people. And many of these health disparities are not correlated with socioeconomic status. The vicious cycle of racism that causes ill health, compounded by more racism, which causes more ill health, is staggeringly fatiguing. Strategies to heal and bounce back from the pain are important but fail to dismantle the systems that cause the pain. We have to come together as a society to find the keys that open the interlocked systems that are so tightly bound in the history of oppression and violence that there seems to be no way to loosen them, let alone unlock them.

It is rare that others see beyond the "-ism vortex" and first recognize my talents. As a person living at the intersection of three marginalized identities, I often wonder where I fall in the political agenda of big decision makers.

—Crystal Emery, filmmaker and writer

FIVE

The Many Layers of Black Fatigue

I remember my uncle Don from when I was growing up. He was my mother's youngest brother (she had two brothers and a sister, Frances, after whom I am named), who had been adopted by the family. "Wayward" was the nice word that was used by other family members to describe him. He ran away from home when he was 16 and had numerous "careers," including that of an evangelical minister for a time. Uncle Don was a drifter, an alcoholic, who would frequently show up on our doorstep, unannounced, always in the middle of the night. Most times he was drunk, incoherent, and destitute. He would stay for a week or maybe even months and then leave as abruptly as he had appeared, and nobody knew where he went or when he would return.

My mother (and, by extension, my father, albeit reluctantly) was the only one in the family who unconditionally supported and defended Uncle Don. Uncle Don always knew that he could find refuge at our house. I was too young initially to understand Uncle Don's story. It was not until I was a teenager that my mother shared with me that Uncle Don was gay. It was never clear to me whether he really ran away from home as a teenager (that was always the story) or whether he was put out because of his sexual orientation. I remember overhearing my other uncles, with whom he had lived growing up, call him all kinds of vile names and pretty much disown him.

I think Uncle Don was in his late 40s when he and Tony started their relationship. Tony was a master chef. I loved going to Toronto, Ontario to visit Uncle Don and Tony because we would be treated to the most amazing gourmet meals. He made the best Caesar salad from scratch. Tony took care of Uncle Don, who, until his death at about age 60, had a drinking problem that resulted in some pretty bizarre behaviors that I will not share here.

I share Uncle Don's story because he was a Black, gay man. His sexual orientation added another stigmatized identity. A stigmatized identity is defined as an identity that is socially devalued with negative stereotypes and beliefs attached to it. Being gay in the late 1950s and 1960s was clearly a shunned identity, and Uncle Don did not really come out until he met Tony. As a matter of fact, I remember him having a girlfriend named Monica for a time. I cannot imagine the emotional turmoil that Uncle Don endured in trying to be who he was in a world where he was rejected—a world that categorized gays as aberrant and homosexuality as something someone needed to be cured of. My aunt Frances was more accepting, like my mother, but she lived with her brothers in an extended-family situation and Uncle Don could not go home. He was not able to navigate his two stigmatized identities very well and died carrying the pain of his family's and society's rejection.

There has long been a belief that Black people, by and large, are antigay. Antigay sentiments in the Black community, as in any community, come from various sources—religion, conceptions of respectability, and heteronormative beliefs. However, since Uncle Don's generation, attitudes have shifted significantly. According to a 2019 Pew Research study, 62 percent of whites support same-sex marriage, as do 58 percent of Hispanics and 51 percent of Blacks.[1] Almost 70 percent of Black people oppose policies that would allow businesses to refuse services to LGBTQ individuals.[2] The message today from Black leaders is that Black people are no more homophobic than any other group. While this is somewhat reassuring, the fact that a higher percentage of Blacks than whites disapprove of gay marriage means that Black LGBTQ individuals are still more likely to carry the stress of an intragroup stigmatized identity, which can be even more stressful when those close to you do not accept you.

Even though homosexuality is not as stigmatized as it was 50 years ago, according to a 2019 Yale University School of Public Health study, 83 percent of the world's LGBTQ population is still closeted.[3] According to the authors of the study, "Concealment takes its toll through the stress of hiding and also because it can keep sexual minorities away from each other and from adequate public health attention. But in many places around the world, concealment and its stressors are safer than the alternative."

Forty-six percent of the LGBTQ community in the United States remains closeted in the workplace, compared with 50 percent in 2008.[4] They carry the daily stress of accidentally saying something that would reveal their sexual orientation or gender identity. Trying to manage all of this can lead to lower productivity and performance and ultimately job loss. The Supreme Court only ruled in June 2020 that the LGBTQ community is covered under the Civil Rights Act of 1964, which makes employment discrimination illegal.[5] Before that ruling, only 21 states and the District of Columbia had such legislation.

My friend and colleague Judith Katz,[6] a thought leader in diversity, developed a list of heterosexual privileges. I have adapted a few here to point out what causes fatigue for those who identify as other than heterosexual.

- I can hold hands, touch, and dance with the person I love in public without *fear* of others' reactions.
- I can share openly with colleagues, friends, and family the news of falling in love, anniversaries, details of vacations, or what I did last weekend.
- I can talk about the person I love without *fear* of losing my job.
- I can keep pictures of the person I love on my desk without *fear* of reprisal, harassment, or being accused of flaunting my sexuality.
- If I am considered for a work transfer, the company will often support me in finding employment for my significant other.
- I will not be discriminated against in finding a place to live.
- I do not have to be subjected to jokes and slurs and outright hatred on a daily basis because of my sexual orientation.
- I do not *fear* being turned away from my house of worship because of whom I love.

- I do not have to live my life in secret, lie to people I love, or *fear* being rejected and condemned by my parents or family.
- I do not have to *fear* that I will be attacked or beaten because of whom I love.

I italicized the word "fear" to highlight it as the recurring emotion. In chapter 4, I shared the relationship of fear to health outcomes. Fear is often compounded when you live with more than one stigmatized identity.

Race, Sexual Orientation or Gender Identity, Religion, and Citizenship

Race and sexual orientation are just two permutations of intersectionality, a term coined by Kimberlé Crenshaw,[7] professor at both Columbia Law School and the University of California, Los Angeles, originally to address the perpetual exclusion of Black women in feminist, antiracist discourse. The definition now takes on a broader meaning. Intersectionality recognizes that group identities, such as race, gender, sexuality, class, religion, ability, citizenship or immigration status, age, and so on, overlap and intersect in dynamic ways that shape and continually reshape an individual's experience. There are multiple forms of privilege and oppression based on the various combinations. My uncle Don is an example of just one such combination that serves to compound Black fatigue.

During one of The Winters Group's Engaging in Bold, Inclusive Conversations trainings, one of the participants shared that he is gay, a Muslim, and from the Middle East. He said, "This is three strikes against me. When I wait for the train at the metro, I don't stand near the edge in fear that someone might push me into an oncoming train." His fear stemmed from an incident reported on the news in which a person was arrested for attempting to do just that as she shouted, "I hate all Muslims and want to kill them."

Let us consider the experience of seeking medical care as someone who is Black, poor, and identifies as nonbinary. "Nonbinary," also referred to as genderqueer, is a spectrum of gender identities that are not exclusively masculine or feminine—identities that are outside the gender binary of male-female. Chapter 4 chronicles the health disparities that exist for people who are visibly Black. Now compound this with gender identities that are not even understood by many in the medical profession. For example, intake forms and medical records might not allow gender options other than male or female, which leads to misgendering nonbinary patients. Such patients then must educate medical staff, which can be a fatiguing, stressful experience. Research shows that at least 25 percent of those who identify as nonbinary avoid seeking treatment because they fear discrimination based on gender identity.[8] Now add the fear of discrimination based on race and this exponentially increases the stress that can lead to trauma and inequitable life experiences and outcomes.

In November 2019, the Human Rights Campaign issued a report entitled *A National Epidemic: Fatal Anti-transgender Violence in the United States in 2019*. The annual report revealed that between January and November 2019, at least 22 transgender and gender-nonconforming people were killed in the United States, and all but one were Black. Also, since January 2013, the Human Rights Campaign has documented more than 150 transgender and gender-nonconforming people who were victims of fatal violence; at least 127 (84 percent) were people of color. "Transgender women of color are living in crisis, especially Black transgender women. The toxic intersection of racism, sexism, transphobia and easy access to guns conspire to deny so many members of the transgender and gender non-conforming community access to housing, employment and other necessities to survive and thrive."[9]

Race, Sex, Parental Status, and Income

Imagine that a single Black mother with three children, classified as low income, is looking for a place to live. Her race, gender, income, and single motherhood are all stigmatized identities that layer to create multiple opportunities for fatigue from trying to navigate unjust systems. Chapter 3 points out that redlining is still an issue for Black people, limiting the choices of where we can live. And low-income people pay at least 50 percent of their salaries in housing costs, compared with 33 percent for those not living in poverty.[10] Compounding that, poor Black women are evicted at higher rates than poor men. "Black men are locked up and Black women are locked out" is how a study by the MacArthur Foundation put it. It analyzed evictions in Milwaukee, where Black women were 9.6 percent of the population and 30 percent of the evictions. Low wages and children were two contributing factors. The researchers also found that men were more likely to confront landlords and dare them to go through eviction proceedings, while women avoided the landlord, explaining that the eviction notice terrified them. The researchers called out the gender dynamic at play. Men often agree to perform other services such as maintenance around the building in lieu of rent. Women tend to just try to avoid the landlord.[11] Women with young children who are already working low-wage jobs do not have the time or energy to perform other services, and too often the other service that the landlord demands is "sex for rent." Eviction sets off a series of other consequences that increase stress and fatigue. Evictees often lose their possessions. If they can keep their possessions, they may incur storage fees. The children may have to change schools. Legal evictions include a court record, which can affect a family's ability to find acceptable alternate housing. An eviction can also lead to job loss because of the time away from work to address the situation. Studies also show that eviction can affect a mother's mental health, with higher rates of depression reported as long as two years after the move. The above mentioned MacArthur Foundation Study asserts "Eviction is not just a condition of poverty; it is a cause of it."[12] In addition to Milwaukee, other areas that have disproportionate eviction rates include Richmond; North Charleston, South Carolina; Hampton, Virginia; Newport News, Virginia; and Jackson, Mississippi.[13]

Not only do poor Black mothers have difficulties with housing, studies show that they struggle more to find affordable childcare than white people. Federal programs such as the Child Care and Development Block Grant and Head Start, targeted toward low-income families with young children, only fund about 15 percent of eligible families, and the subsidy amount is too low to support the cost of high-quality childcare.[14] Faced with the prospect of continuing to work for low wages and not being able to afford childcare and adequate housing, quitting your job and applying for public assistance may be your last resort. If you make this choice, yet another stigma will be added to your identity—welfare mother or welfare "queen," which carries stereotypes of being lazy and unmotivated. While we thought that this characterization had subsided from when it was popularly spouted during the Reagan era, President Donald Trump signed an executive order in 2018 requiring recipients of federal aid in housing, food, and health care to be employed to receive aid. The order is interpreted by social justice advocates as an attempt by the administration to purge the assistance rolls by forcing out people they believe are taking advantage of the system.[15] The requirements ignore important systemic barriers to employment, such as housing, transportation, childcare, and other medical and social barriers.

If you can empathize, perhaps you can feel the stress and even trauma associated with navigating systems that intentionally or unintentionally discriminate against every one of your salient identities. It is fatiguing.

Race, Sex, and Disability

Crystal Emery is a filmmaker and writer. She identifies as an African American female with a disability—she is a wheelchair-riding quadriplegic. She writes in a 2016 *Time* online piece,[16] "I exist as a triple threat to our society's normative conceptions (white, male, able-bodied)." She says that she never knows what people see first: her disability, her Blackness, or her gender. "It is rare that others see beyond the '-ism vortex' and first recognize my talents." She goes on to say, "As a person living at the intersection of three marginalized identities, I often wonder where I fall in the political agenda of big decision makers."

Emery's creative work is routinely challenged with questions like, "Did someone make the film for you?" or "Did someone else write this article?" The stereotype that many people have of someone who looks like her is that she has limited capabilities. She says she is left wondering, Do they question my talent because I am Black? A woman? Or someone in a wheelchair? I can't imagine how fatiguing it is for her to have to contend with such questions.

SUMMARY

Living with layers of marginalized identities can exponentially increase Black fatigue, creating one insurmountable obstacle after another. These experiences often lead to internalized oppression, described in chapter 2, which leads to the physiological and psychological ills described in chapter 4.

We must be more aware and acknowledge the layers of identities that compound fatigue. Black people need to be self-aware of the intersections and address each identity separately as well as in combination. This can be difficult, triggering, and, yes, fatiguing. Seeking support for stress and trauma from professionals who are equipped to address the layers of identities may be helpful. If professional help is not accessible, talking with trusted friends who may share the same identities or seeking out healing circles or other support groups, as described in chapter 4, may be useful.

We must stop the one-identity approach of addressing racism. We all have multiple identities, and Black people almost always have more than one marginalized identity—Black and female; Black and gay; Black and poor. And as described in this chapter, we might be navigating more than two marginalized identities. There are many different combinations of intersections that can potentially increase Black fatigue.

The next three chapters explore Black fatigue for those who identify as Black women, Black men, and Black children. I thought it important to talk about intersectionality first and then share how fatigue plays out at the intersection of the two most visible identities—race and gender for Black men and Black women—and lastly how it manifests in Black children.

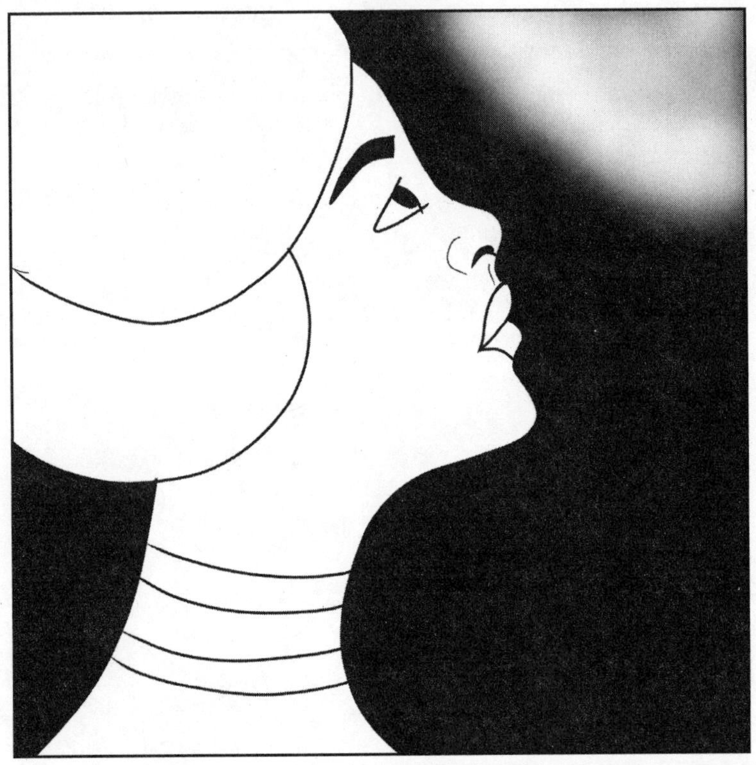

The most disrespected person in America is the Black woman. The most unprotected person in America is the Black woman. The most neglected person in America is the Black woman.

—Malcolm X, Black Muslim minister
and civil rights activist

SIX

Say Her Name: Black Women's Fatigue

Malcolm X's assessment has not changed since 1962 when he famously uttered these words. I live at the intersection of Blackness and womanhood. This intersection is fraught with its own unique manifestations of fatigue, some of which I have pointed out in previous chapters.

I shared in the introduction that as a cisgender, heterosexual, college-educated, able-bodied, middle-class Black woman I am in many ways privileged. I do not claim to have lived the experiences of my similarly hued sisters. I speak from my life and do not represent all who identify as Black women. I know that there are similarities from decades of relationships with Black women from different walks of life, and the stories we share with each other often carry similar threads. They are messages of pride and power often juxtaposed to deep feelings of self-doubt and helplessness. They are stories of achieving against all odds and stories of exasperation from not being able to find our way out of the perpetual maze of anti-Black racism unique to Black women. They are stories of faith, strength, resilience, and hope along with stories of neglect, abuse, and violence. They are stories of passion and "magic" against a backdrop of labels like "angry" and "less innocent." Black women have amassed a treasure trove of wisdom from living with our identities, but too often our voices are silenced, ignored, or denied.

Even with these shared experiences, no two of us are exactly alike. I offer my stories and those of several other Black women in this chapter, acknowledging that this does not scratch the surface of characterizing who and what we are.

Beyond our skin color and often hair texture, what do Black women in the United States have in common? We know from chapter 4 that as a group we suffer disproportionately in health outcomes.

Black women also share a greater likelihood of being incarcerated (twice as likely as white women)[1] and killed by law enforcement (1.3 times more likely), and they are more likely to live in poverty (21 percent of Black women versus 9.7 percent of white women),[2] never marry (50 percent versus 33 percent for white women), be single mothers (54 percent), and fare worse in the workplace (underemployed and underpaid), all issues discussed in this chapter.

Sister Marjorie's Story

Sister Marjorie, as she was affectionately called, was my sister-in-law. She was the sister of my late husband, whom I referenced in chapter 1. I loved her like a sister and marveled at her heart full of grace that never wavered, even in the wake of numerous challenges. Sister Marjorie identified as a Black woman. She passed away recently at age 67 after a seven-year battle with breast cancer. I don't feel that I am exaggerating when I say that she lived her life in a way that would qualify her for sainthood. She embodied unwavering faith, strength, humility, intelligence, service, and resilience. Married young, she birthed four children in the span of 6 years, and even though she was married for 17 years before divorcing, her husband was in and out of the household during that time, providing inconsistent financial support to the family. They often lived at the front door of poverty.

Sister Marjorie grew up in urban Washington, DC, in the 1960s along with her four siblings, including my late husband, Joe, reared by a low-income single mother. Raised as a devout Catholic, Sister Marjorie even considered becoming a nun but wanted children. She converted to Islam in the early 1970s, attracted by its messages of self-love and liberation, and made the pilgrimage to Mecca five times. Life was not easy for Marjorie and her children. She had left college after her freshman year to marry. However, despite financial constraints, she was committed to being there for her children without giving up her dream of finishing her college education. Without a driver's license or car, she returned to college part time in 1981 and made straight As while also tutoring students in computer programming. She completed her bachelor's degree within five years and landed a project manager job with Bell South (which later became AT&T), from where she retired in 2015.

In her obituary, written by one of her daughters, Jamillah, who graduated with honors with an electrical engineering degree from Duke University and later a PhD in Islamic studies, she says of her mother:

> She walked distances with us to catch the bus because she didn't have a car. And when she finally did get one, she offered ride after ride to sisters in need. After saving to buy a house, she struggled to manage the needed repairs. She taught us to obey Allah, reminding us when we failed, holding us through the hardships, and lifting us when we turned back to God. My mother treated strangers as they were old friends, providing warm beds and unforgettable meals for extended family and new acquaintances. I remember her loading tables and trays of food into her car, even when she was ill, to transport to the homeless. Truly, in her deepest suffering, she did everything in her power to lighten the burdens of others, until she just couldn't do it anymore.

Her four children, now all professionally successful, inherited the spirit of giving and service from their mother. When her youngest son committed robbery as a teenager, she was the one who turned him into authorities and then faithfully made the two-hour trip to visit him every other week for 15 years so that he would never forget that he was still loved. As a result of unsuccessful appeals for an early release based on good behavior, he served the entire sentence.

Within the Muslim community, she founded organizations to uplift youths and feed the hungry. My fondest memories of Sister Marjorie are our loving and engaging conversations in her kitchen as I watched her prepare meals for the homeless. She worked tirelessly, never complaining, in service of others and loved everyone in her path unconditionally. She never complained of being fatigued, but I know that she was.

To one degree or another, Sister Marjorie's story is the story of many Black women. I know and have known many Sister Marjories who have simultaneously faced poverty and found themselves as single mothers attempting to protect their children while instilling strong values. I know others who have supported someone close who has been incarcerated, and others who have faced life-threatening diseases like cancer. Like Sister Marjorie, many of us are strong in our faith, as I mentioned in chapter 4. And many of us earnestly believe that it is our purpose to serve those in need, to give back, to share, to sacrifice, to care as much about others as we do ourselves, all without complaint and as best as possible, without letting the fatigue imperil us.

Say Her Name

As mentioned in chapter 3, Black women also are disproportionately targeted by law enforcement; however, these incidents receive little media attention. Black women are disproportionately killed, raped, and subjected to inhumane treatment. This lack of coverage was painfully evident when Nancy Grace, a former prosecutor turned media personality, reported on missing women. All of the women Grace reported about were white, and the obvious lack of coverage about missing Black women led the late PBS *NewsHour* anchor Gwen Ifill to coin the phrase "missing White woman syndrome" to describe the media's exclusive focus on white women.

Even with the new focus on police killings of Black people, it is still difficult to find the stories about any of the known Black women mentioned in SayHerName reports.[3] The SayHerName movement was started by the African American Policy Forum with a report coauthored by Andrea J. Ritchie and Kimberlé Crenshaw. Ritchie is a lawyer and activist for women of color, and Crenshaw is a full-time professor at the University of California, Los Angeles, School of Law and Columbia Law School known for introducing the concept of intersectionality specific to the intersection of race and gender. I referenced Crenshaw in chapter 5. The concept emerged from three legal cases that Crenshaw critiqued in a 1989 paper[4] dealing with the issues of both racial discrimination and sex discrimination. The court had decided that efforts that combine both racial discrimination and sex discrimination claims were not valid. The judge ruled against the plaintiffs, saying that Black women could not be considered a separate, protected class within the law, or else it would risk opening a "Pandora's box" of minorities who would demand to be heard based on intersections.

Years later, in 2015, the *Say Her Name: Resisting Police Brutality against Black Women* report was published, with the goal of bringing attention to the incidents involving Black women who are not often given the same spotlight as Black men. The report gathers stories of Black women who have been killed by police and who have experienced gender-specific forms of police violence and provides some analytical frames for understanding their experiences. Despite being 7 percent of the population, Black women have accounted for 20 percent of the unarmed people killed by police since 1999.[5] Breonna Taylor's 2020 murder by the police, mentioned in the preface, garned widespread attention along with the Ahmaud Arbery and George Floyd killings, which happened around the same time and sparked the Black Lives Matter protests.

Stand by Your Man

Black women experience domestic violence at higher rates than white women. According to the Blackburn Center, 40 percent of Black women will experience domestic violence in their lifetime, compared with 31 percent of white women, and are 2.5 times more likely to be killed by their partner than white women, causing the Black Women's Health Project to declare domestic violence the number one health issue facing Black women.[6] I explore the reasons for these disturbing statistics in chapter 7. I know women who have left abusive relationships. I know women who have stayed in abusive relationships. Black women are taught that they should protect Black men and boys at all costs. According to Tricia B. Bent-Goodley, professor of social work at Howard University, "Black women have been found to withstand abuse, subordinate feelings and concerns with safety, and make a conscious self-sacrifice for what is perceived as the greater good of the community, but to their own physical, psychological and spiritual detriment."[7]

The reasons for the disturbing level of abuse and violence are complex and are captured by Joy DeGruy in *Post Traumatic Slave Syndrome*. She says, "The enslavement experience was one of continued violent attacks on the mind, body and spirit. Men, women and children were traumatized throughout their lives and the violent attacks during slavery persisted long after emancipation. In the face of these injuries, those traumatized adapted their attitudes and behaviors in order to simply survive and these adaptations continue to manifest today."[8]

Strong Faith

Black women are more likely than Black men to turn to their faith to cope with abuse, racism, and sexism. While Black men and women are both more religious than white men and women, according to a Pew Research survey, 80 percent of Black women answered that religion was very important to them, compared with 69 percent of Black men. Moreover, 78 percent of Black men believe in God with absolute certainty, versus 86 percent of Black women.[9] Results from a study published in the *Journal for the Scientific Study of Religion* show that religious guidance and being active with a religious community moderate the effects of racism on psychological distress, offsetting but not buffering the effects of discrimination.[10]

"Just pray on it" is often the advice that Black women give each other and others to deal with their life's burdens. Strong belief in an omnipotent, omniscient, omnipresent God who would never leave us or forsake us is how many of us endure. The Black church is a place of refuge where you know your Blackness is unconditionally accepted; you are uplifted and supported and leave Sunday service with the strength to survive another week. "Faith without works is dead" (James 2:26). It is the combination of our faith and persistent work for justice that has brought us this far. Black women are able to thrive in spite of centuries of denigration.

Black Women and Body Image

As in every other aspect of society, dominant culture defines beauty too. The Western world has a Eurocentric concept of beauty—thin, white or very light skin, long hair (preferably blond), and blue eyes. During slavery, Black women's bodies were violated, and negative images surfaced of Black women as hypersexualized breeders whom slave owners used to populate their slave stock. The historical image of Black women in media was either that of an overweight "mammy" or that of a hypersexual "Jezebel." During the 2020 Black Lives Matter protests for racial justice, Quaker Oats decided to discontinue its 130-year-old stereotypical Aunt Jemima mammy imagery and branding.[11]

Halle Berry is still the only Black woman to win an Oscar (2001) for Best Actress for her performance in *Monster's Ball.* Some critics say that it was not her best performance and that it exploited the stereotype of the hypersexualized Black woman. Angela Bassett publicly stated that she turned down the role for that reason.

By and large, Black women do not fit the image of the dominant view of beauty. African features are considered ugly and less desirable. Michelle Obama and former Obama aide Valerie Jarrett have been likened to apes. In addition, Black women, unlike white women, are rarely characterized as feminine or delicate and needing protection. In chapter 8 I discuss how the perception of needing less protection starts during childhood.

There are a number of high-profile examples of "body shaming" directed at Black women. Here are three examples. When tennis phenom Serena Williams sported a catsuit-type outfit, it was banned by the French Open even though Anne White wore a similar outfit in 1985. White's body type was thin, in contrast to Williams's thick, curvy body type. Serena and her sister Venus have been subjected to numerous comments in the media about their body types. Misty Copeland was the first African American woman to be named principal dancer at the American Ballet Theatre, but when she was 13, she was turned down by a ballet academy for having the wrong body type—too muscular. Popular singer Lizzo, who has built a reputation for her unapologetic and positive body imaging and self-love messages, has been body shamed by fitness enthusiasts for her plus-size body type.

Even though 80 percent of Black women are classified as overweight according to body mass index standards,[12] based on a number of studies, Black women are satisfied with their bodies and are motivated to lose weight based on health-related concerns, not Western standards of beauty.[13] As a matter of fact, intraculturally, larger body frames are more often viewed positively than negatively. It is considered a compliment when a Black woman is described as "thick and curvy." It is the white world (dominant culture) that has stamped "bad" on plus-size women. Beyoncé was recently criticized by the Black community for excluding plus sizes in her new line of athletic clothing, the Adidas X Ivy Park collection.

Another important example of the criticism of Black women for their looks is the controversy over natural hair. Based on a study conducted by Cornell University School of Industrial and Labor Relations students in 2016, while the corporate world "accepts" women with natural hair, it is considered less professional, especially by white women.[14] I shared my hair experience from the 1970s in chapter 1. Then is now—in 2019, there were media accounts that actress Gabrielle Union was fired from *America's Got Talent* after she reported racist remarks by show leaders. She said that she was also told on numerous occasions that her hairstyles were too Black.[15] In the introduction, I mentioned the CROWN Act, recent legislation that was needed to protect the rights of Black people to wear our hair in its natural state as a result of numerous incidents over recent years in which schools and workplaces have attempted to ban such styles. This type of oppression is an example of white supremacy. As fatiguing is the all-too-common question asked by white people, "Can I touch your hair?" The stress associated with perhaps wanting to preserve the relationship with the inquirer while at the same time needing to correct this microaggression as totally inappropriate on several levels is yet something else that many Black women have to deal with as a part of their day-to-day journey.

Colorism is another issue for Black women. Lighter skin is often seen as "better than" dark skin, even intragroup. White and Black people are more favorably disposed toward people with lighter skin, rating them as smarter, wealthier, and happier in surveys. Black people used to discriminate against each other by denying membership to certain organizations if one could not pass the brown paper bag test. While colorism affects all Black people, intragroup, it is more prominent for women as Black women often perceive darker-skinned Black men as more desirable. The skin-lightening industry for women is estimated to be over $10 billion globally. Attention to this bias has mitigated it over the years and it is now more common to see dark-skinned Black women being included in the spectrum of what constitutes beauty, such as South Sudanese model Nyakim Gatwech, who was nonetheless told in 2016 by an Uber driver to bleach her skin.

Black Women and the Workforce

Black women, on average, earn sixty-two cents to every dollar that a white man earns. White women make eighty-two cents to every dollar a white man earns.[16] The higher level of education does not change the wage gaps. Among doctorate degree holders, for instance, Black women earn 60 percent of what white men do, and white women earn 7 percent more than Black women.[17]

The median annual income for Black women is $34,008, compared with $42,484 for white women and $61,576 for white men.[18] As mentioned in chapter 3, the net worth of a single Black woman without a bachelor's degree is $500 and with a bachelor's degree is $5,000.

In February 2019, the Economic Policy Institute posted a blog entry that started with this statement: "The black woman's experience in America provides arguably the most overwhelming evidence of the persistent and ongoing drag from gender and race discrimination on the economic fate of workers and families."[19] The post asserts that since slavery, Black women have fared the worst in the labor market because of discriminatory practices, as well as demeaning perceptions of Black women and their role. Black women have been perceived as "workers" and not women who might choose to stay at home with children as white women did.

In 1880, 35.4 percent of married Black women and 73.3 percent of single Black women were in the labor force, compared with only 7.3 percent of married white women and 23.8 percent of single white women. These differences extended into the 1970s, when, even after marriage, white women would typically exit the labor force. Black women were forced to stay in the labor market, not just because it was an expectation but also because Black men could not find adequate employment (forced to take lower-paying, less stable jobs) because of discrimination and therefore Black women, often in domestic roles, became co-breadwinners in married households. Today over 80 percent of Black mothers are the primary breadwinners for their families, compared with 50 percent of white women.[20]

Black women have been and continue to be overrepresented in low-wage jobs with fewer legal protections. As an example, the Social Security Act of 1935 primarily excluded Black women until the 1960s. Caseworkers denied most poor Black women cash assistance under the act because they expected Black women to be employed mothers and not stay-at-home moms like white women. The New Deal minimum wage, overtime pay, and collective bargaining legislation excluded the main sectors where

Black women worked—domestic service and farming. Corrections have been made since then, but there are still gaps that disadvantage Black women. Moreover, Black women continue to be overrepresented in low-paying jobs that do not provide benefits such as sick pay, health insurance, maternity leave, and retirement plans. For example, 36 percent of Black women workers have jobs that do not provide paid sick leave,[21] compounding the health issues highlighted in chapter 4. These inequities were highlighted during the 2020 coronavirus pandemic. Black women were more likely to be in essential jobs that put them at greater risk of contracting the virus or in nonessential jobs where they faced furloughs or layoffs.

Workplace Experiences

Study after study confirms that Black women face a great deal of racism and sexism in the workplace. Navigating the intersection of race and gender in work environments with deep-seated cultural biases is fatiguing. Whether we work in an entry-level job or have made it into leadership, our identities as Black women shape narratives that are very different from those of other identity groups. For example, stereotypes that Black women must overcome in workplace include being aggressive, opinionated, and angry. We are criticized for our appearance, as pointed out earlier in this chapter. As I highlighted in chapter 1, when I was in the corporate world, I spent a lot of time trying not to be too aggressive, yet assertive enough so as not to be labeled too passive; both are characterizations that I received. As previously mentioned, I was told that I should straighten my hair when I sported a short Afro style. The fatigue of trying to change myself to fit some archetype of the corporate culture led me to leave

Black women
Source: The Winters Group, Inc. Art by Krystle Nicholas.

the company. According to a survey by the Center for Talent Innovation, 36 percent of Black women said they intend to leave their current employment, versus 27 percent of white women.[22]

The "angry Black woman" is probably the most fatiguing stereotype to manage. I contend that as Black women we have a lot to be angry about. Brittany J. Harris, vice president of learning and innovation at The Winters Group, put it this way in a post in our Inclusion Solution newsletter. "I find it fascinating how I've essentially learned (internalized) that suppressing my feelings, truth, and anger (despite how much studies show this can be a detriment to my health) is worth not being characterized as or associated with being an 'Angry Black Woman.'" She goes on to ask, "What is wrong with anger? Anger is a very real and valid feeling. It is (or should be) an acceptable response to mistreatment and discrimination. It has been proven to be a powerful channel for action, change, and impact."[23]

Expressing anger may lead to tone policing: *If only you had said it with less anger, maybe you would have been heard.* We have been socialized not to show too much emotion in the workplace, fearing that we will be negatively labeled. Continually suppressing authentic emotions is fatiguing and bad for our health. Those who are tempted to tone police, might pay more attention to the root of the anger rather than their discomfort with the tone.

These experiences can lead to internalized oppression, which is when we believe the negative stereotypes about our group that have been perpetuated by the dominant group. I think internalized oppression is more common than we know because there is little research on its widespread impact on feelings of self-doubt, its erosion of self-esteem and self-worth, and its generation of helplessness and hopelessness. Internalized oppression generated by systemic racism can lead to a feeling of needing constantly to be on guard and increase stress levels.

A 2018 report by Catalyst, an organization that researches workplace experiences for women, titled *Day-to-Day Experiences of Emotional Tax among Women and Men of Color in the Workplace*[24] found that as a result of, or in anticipation of, unfair treatment, professionals of color report a high number of instances of being "on guard" to protect themselves against racial and gender bias, causing what they describe as an emotional tax. An emotional tax is the combination of feeling different from peers at work because of gender, race, or ethnicity and the associated effects on health, well-being, and ability to thrive at work.[25]

Of the 1,569 professionals surveyed for the study, researchers found that across the board, more than half of all women of any given background reported being highly on guard. Black women led the group, with 58 percent saying that they felt on guard throughout their professional lives, followed by 56 percent of Latinas, 52 percent of multiracial women, and 51 percent of Asian women.

"Women of color continue to deal with some of the workplace's most entrenched hurdles, such as pay inequities and near invisibility in top leadership roles, as well as daunting roadblocks that stifle the meaningful dialogue that would help make real progress," according to the study authors. "Over time, these daily battles take a heavy toll on women of color, creating a damaging link between their health and the workplace."[26] Asian, Black, and Latinx respondents who reported higher levels of being on guard were also more likely to report sleep problems (58 percent) than those with lower levels of being on guard (12 percent).[27]

Confirming the results from the Catalyst study, Lean In and McKinsey and Company conduct an annual report on women in the workplace. According to the 2019 report, Black women continue to experience the worst workplace outcomes. For example, Black women are much less likely than any other group to feel they have an equal opportunity to grow and advance, that the best opportunities go to the most deserving employees, and that they are supported by their managers. They also report that they are less happy at work and more likely to leave their company than white women.[28] This and other studies confirm that Black women are likely to report being just as ambitious as white women, if not more so, desiring higher-level roles in their organizations, but they are the least likely to be promoted. Black women represent 18 percent of the professional workforce, according to the Lean In and McKinsey and Company study, but occupy only 4 percent of the C-suite, compared with 30 percent and 18 percent for white women. The frustration of being passed over again and again is fatiguing and leads to a higher number of Black women leaving the corporate world and striking out on their own like I did. According to *Inc.* magazine,[29] the number of white women–owned businesses grew 40 percent from 1997 to 2016, while those owned by Black and Hispanic women showed growth rates at 518 percent and 452 percent, respectively.

Black women (and men—see chapter 7) face daily microaggressions at work, defined as brief, sometimes subtle, everyday comments that either consciously or unconsciously disparage others based on their personal characteristics or perceived group membership.[30] Three categories of microaggressions that can occur in everyday interactions are microassaults, microinsults, and microinvalidations. While "microaggressions" is the commonly used and understood term, I believe that the impact can be "macro" on Black people, not "micro." I thus suggest we drop "micro" and call them aggressions.

~~Micro~~assaults: Conscious, deliberate, and either subtly or explicitly biased attitudes, beliefs, or behaviors that are communicated to marginalized groups through verbalizations or behaviors.

- "Why are you so angry?"
- "Why do you people always play the race card?"
- "You have so much passion. Maybe you need to tone it down for the meeting."
- "I don't think that hair style is appropriate for work."

- "You are pretty for a dark-skinned girl."
- "You are different [meaning from another Black woman]."
- "We had a Black woman a few years ago in our department. She was really nice, but it did not work out."

~~Micro~~insults: Interpersonal communications that convey stereotypes, rudeness, and insensitivity and that demean a person's identity. Unlike ~~micro~~assaults, ~~micro~~insults are often committed unconsciously and may seem more subtle.

- "You are so articulate."
- Encountering mispronunciation of one's name over and over again.
- "Can I touch your hair?"
- "What is the Black woman's perspective on this?"
- Encountering an expression of surprise that you are in your role ("Oh, you're the manager"—either a look of surprise or verbalization of it).
- "I have a good friend who is Black."

~~Micro~~invalidations: Communication cues that exclude, negate, or nullify the thoughts, feelings, or experiential realities of certain groups.

- Mansplaining/whitesplaining: when a man or white woman explains to a Black woman her own experience.
- Having one's input ignored and the same idea accepted from a white person.
- Being mistaken for the other Black woman (we all look alike syndrome).

- "You should be proud of how far your people have come."
- Being constantly excluded from meeting invites where you should be included.
- Being ignored in meetings (invisibility).
- Defensiveness ("I had that happen to me too").

~~Micro~~aggressions in the workplace are fatiguing to manage on a daily basis. When do you let them go? When do you speak up? What is the interpretation on the part of the aggressor—that you are being too sensitive? Will it affect your career chances if you say something?

Chief Counselor and Consoler Fatigue

Black women are often de facto chief counselors and consolers for other Black people in the workplace. Often there are so few Black people of influence in the organization that newer or lower-level hires do not know whom to turn to when they need to bare their souls about their less-than-inclusive experiences. My daughter had a chief counselor and consoler when she was in corporate America, another Black woman with whom she could share her frustrations. Once she retired, my daughter's days were numbered in the corporate world.

In higher education, Black women professors, in particular, find themselves counseling students who are not even in their classes. In the business world, accounts of younger Black professionals seeking support from more seasoned employees are not uncommon. And if your formal role relates to diversity, equity, and inclusion in the organization, it takes its toll when you are not able to change systems for the better. The chief counselor and consoler role adds to the emotional burden and is fatiguing.

On Every Diversity Committee Fatigue

Black women and Black men are fatigued by being tokenized. As an example, we are often tapped for every committee that has "diversity" in the name. For some reason white people think that diversity, by default, means you pick the Black person. Recently, a client was sharing the list of people the company was selecting for a newly formed diversity committee, and the names she read mostly sounded like Black, Latino, or Asian ones. I asked how many white males would be on the committee, and she kept naming the same names. She thought I did not want white men on the committee and said, We only have four. Is that OK? When I explained that I asked because the committee should not just be people of color and women, she was surprised.

Black women who serve on these committees do it in addition to their functional responsibilities and attempts to balance work and life. It is most often uncompensated. Leaders should consider the additional labor (emotional and physical) needed to serve in these capacities and fairly compensate. It is fatiguing to be overworked, and it is even more fatiguing not to be compensated for it.

A Strained Sisterhood: Black Women and White Women

The archetype of "Karen" has recently become a popular meme to describe middle-aged white women who exploit their privilege, entitlement, and racism. "Karen" incidents that have gone viral on the internet, showing white women challenging Black people's right to be where they are and doing what they are doing. For example, demanding to know if a family has the right to be barbecuing in a public park or building a deck in their yard or the right to be stenciling Black Lives Matter in chalk on their own property. Often, "Karen" calls 911 and/or claims that she is being physically assaulted. Amy Cooper's Central Park attack against Christian Cooper, the bird watcher, referenced earlier, is a prime example of a "Karen" incident.

Throughout my career, my most difficult interpersonal relationships have been with white women who tend to minimize, patronize, and sympathize rather than empathize or acknowledge the differences that exist between us.

In 2001, academics Ella Edmonson Bell and Stella Nkomo wrote the book *Our Separate Ways: Black and White Women and the Struggle for Professional Identity*,[31] a seminal work that put a spotlight on how Black women's and white women's work experiences differ. Even though gender is the common denominator, race and class were found in their research to drive wedges between us. They found that white women, even if unwittingly, more often aligned themselves with white men. Some 20 years later their findings hold true. The fact that 94 percent of Black women voted for Hillary Clinton and 47 percent of white women voted for Donald Trump in the 2016 presidential election is a prime example of our significantly different worldviews.[32] Today Black women tend not to participate in marches and rallies organized by white women because our unique issues are often minimized or ignored. (History tidbit: While Black women were very active in the struggle for universal suffrage under the Nineteenth Amendment, they were primarily excluded from joining white women's organizations or participating in marches for voting rights.)

Rachel Elizabeth Cargle, who writes and lectures on things that exist at the intersection of race and womanhood, wrote a piece in *Harper's Bazaar* entitled "When White Feminism Is White Supremacy in Heels."[33] She asserts that instead of listening in order to understand the unique experiences of Black women, white women are often more concerned about their feelings and hurt, defined by Robin DeAngelo as white fragility;[34] see any attempts to isolate the issues unique to women of color as disunifying; or resort to the white savior complex ("all the things I have done for Black people").

I recently facilitated a session for a women's leadership program at a large university. As part of the experience, we separated white women and Black women for a 30-minute caucus session. They were assigned a series of questions to explore, including the following:

- How am I viewed as a member of this group?
- How do I experience belonging?
- When am I aware of my group membership?
- How do I experience power as a member of this group?
- What "rules" have been advantageous for me as a member of this group?

Black women shared these observations: They are more apt to be supported by other BIPOC (Black, Indigenous, and other people of color) women than white women; Black women are expected to be strong and not emotional. If a white woman cries, it is taken seriously and "someone's head will roll"; and Oppression Olympics is not uncommon between white women and women of color. Some of the white women were concerned that we had separated the two groups, saying that they thought it would be better to talk about their shared experiences as women. There was an acknowledgment by others that race, especially their white race, is an uncomfortable discussion. They probed, without coming to recommendations, how they could be better allies to women of color, which felt a bit patronizing to me.

In *From Sabotage to Support: A New Vision for Feminist Solidarity in the Workplace*,[35] authors Joy Wiggins and Kami Anderson say that "when white women undermine and dismiss the experiences of BIPOC women, it cuts those women down and takes away their power. It is important to understand the history of feminism and white feminism in particular. . . . The first step is to understand those sabotaging behaviors. Do your work and seek to educate yourself on how you can be a better ally."

Black Woman to Black Woman

White women do not always support us as we would like to be supported, and we do not always support each other as we might. Again, historical racism has influenced this complicated relationship. Since slavery, Black people have been taught that we are inferior, and the intergenerational memory carries this belief on today for many of us.

If your information about Black women comes primarily from reality TV, you might get the impression that Black women do not support each other. We are portrayed as conniving, bitter, contentious, and hating each other. This, from my perspective, is not an accurate portrayal. However, negativity sells.

As with everything related to race, the relationship between Black women is complex. In part, our lack of support for each other is internalized oppression. When we do not feel good about ourselves, we project those feelings onto others like us. Other reasons for a lack of intragroup support in the workplace is self-preservation. Recognizing that Black women comprise two stigmatized identities, there may be an urge to distance ourselves from other Black women so as not to compound the already negative impact of these identities in the workplace. I have heard Black women say that they will not join the Black employee network group because they wish to lessen their identification with their race. Black women are also less likely to join the women's employee network group but for the reason outlined in the previous section.

More than once, I have been told by Black women in a position to hire The Winters Group's services that they had to hire a white organization instead because of "optics"—it might look like giving preferential treatment to a Black-owned company, and there is evidence that people are penalized for advocating for diversity. In a study conducted by David Heckman and colleagues and published in the *Academy of Management Journal* in 2016,[36] they found clear and consistent evidence that women and people of color who promote diversity are penalized in terms of how others perceive their competence and effectiveness. Women and people of color are more apt to come under attack when they speak out for those in their identity group, in a way that white men are not.[37]

Joy DeGruy[38] posits that jealousy and envy within the Black community, leading to the crab-in-the-barrel syndrome, can come from deep-seated beliefs of inferiority. For example, if another Black person is promoted over you and you believe that all Black people are at the bottom of the barrel, so to speak, then this must mean that you are even more inferior—"I am lower than the lowest." If a white person is promoted, while you might think it unfair, it is expected. Navigating these often conflicting and compounding issues is stressful and fatiguing.

Notwithstanding these complexities, I think for the most part Black women are very supportive of each other. We share kindred experiences and often find it fatigue reducing to commiserate about them. I belong to several informal and formal groups for Black women where we can just be, with no judgments or expectations. Many Black women in positions of power have supported The Winters Group over the years without concern about how it would look. I am particularly interested in giving back by offering scholarships and employment and through The Winters Group's social responsibility arm, Live Inclusively Actualized. In the past two years, we have donated over $150,000 to organizations that serve Black women and youths.

#BlackGirlsAreMagic

What do we do to survive and thrive in a world that too often denigrates us? We "keep on keeping on," as my elders used to say. We make sure that the world knows about our "magic." Black Girls Are Magic (abbreviated Black Girl Magic) is a movement that was started by CaShawn Thompson in 2013. "'Black Girl Magic' is a term used to illustrate the universal awesomeness of Black women. It's about celebrating anything we deem particularly dope, inspiring, or mind-blowing about ourselves."[39] This movement, which has gained a huge following of Black women and girls, is designed to counteract all the negative stereotypes about Black women and to create a space where Black girls and women can affirm our power and unique beauty. According to Thompson, "When Black girls and women make the news, breaking barriers and making history, we highlight their accomplishments with these hashtags. When Black girls and women show up, for ourselves and for others, we want the world to know this is who we are and how we have always been. We do not have to be supernatural or superhuman to be magic—we just need to be."[40]

There are a number of companies that are doing more to illustrate Black Girl Magic in their advertising, products, and awards and recognitions. There are more books written by and for Black girls, such as the Doc McStuffins series; there are many more Black dolls to choose from, such as the line from American Girl; and Black women are more often recognized for their work in movie roles that move away from the historical images of mammies and Jezebels, such as Lupita Nyong'o's and Danai Gurira's roles as strong women who chart their own paths in love and war in Disney's *Black Panther* movie.

And, of course, beyond fictional characters, there are strong Black women role models throughout history and today in the likes of Michelle Obama, Oprah Winfrey, Ava DuVernay, Janet Mock (writer, producer, and transgender rights activist), Tarana Burke (who started the Me Too movement), Ruth Carter (costume designer for *Black Panther*), Sheila Johnson (cofounder of Black Entertainment Network and the first Black female billionaire), Venus and Serena Williams, Mae Jemison, and many more household names. And then there are the unsung "Black Girl Magicians" whom we call mamma, big mamma, auntie, sister, grandma, nanna, and a host of other terms of endearment because of the love they gave and the sacrifices they made to influence who we are.

SUMMARY

The compounding and complex conditions and issues that Black women face are especially fatiguing. Black women are stereotyped as "workers" and have internalized this characterization by overachieving, self-sacrificing, and neglecting our health and dismissing the need for self-care. Black women must unapologetically prioritize rest as a part of the movement toward equity and liberation.

We are not looking for saviors. We need authentic support from white women and men in the form of allyship and power brokering. We want our voices to be heard, accepted, and validated, and we want actions to be taken that are specifically intended to dismantle systems of racism for Black women. Some systems are harder to crack than others. Let's tackle one, inequities in pay, because they are tangible, quantifiable, and fixable. If we started there, it would go a long way in eradicating other forms of injustice.

There is no Black woman archetype. Each of us is unique, coming from myriad circumstances with an infinite number of lived experiences. And even though we have been disproportionately used and abused throughout history, we have made and continue to make groundbreaking contributions to society. And we want you to know that we are fatigued from the struggle *and* we are asking you to listen to our call for justice and equity *and* despite it all, we are unstoppable.

I am a man of substance, of flesh and bone, fiber and liquids—and I might even be said to possess a mind. I am invisible, understand, simply because people refuse to see me.

—Ralph Ellison, American novelist, literary critic, and scholar best known for his novel *Invisible Man*

SEVEN

"I Can't Breathe": Black Men's Fatigue

Ralph Ellison, a Black novelist and activist, wrote *Invisible Man* in 1952.[1] The protagonist, a nameless Black man, lives in a racist existence where his personal identity is meaningless. Set in the South in the 1920s and Harlem in the 1930s, the book describes how the invisible man wrestles with the cognitive dissonance of better opportunity and the indignities of racism. As a Black man, he is perceived by dominant society as a collection of negative stereotypes rather than a whole thinking, feeling human. The invisible man says, "They see only my surroundings, themselves, or figments of their imagination—indeed, everything and anything except me."[2] This helps to explain police brutality against Black men. They are killing a collection of stereotypes. The perpetrators refuse to see real, living, breathing people because the anti-Black racism directed toward Black men is so entrenched in their psyches. Not much has changed since Ellison wrote *Invisible Man*.

Ryon's Story

Ryon is a renaissance Black man. He has a bachelor's degree in human resources but prefers to work with his hands. When I met him, he worked for a local heating and air-conditioning contractor by day and by night performed other services such as hanging pictures, installing and wall-mounting smart TVs, cleaning gutters, or just about any other household repair or task you might need. He proudly declares, "I do everything!" Ryon works 12–14 hours a day, 6 days a week. He sometimes brings his preteen sons on the job to teach them the trade (and like most kids their age, they are less than enthusiastic about their father's work). One time he even brought his toddler daughter with him because his wife had to work. Our conversations always turned to his desire to be on his own—to start his own business. He would pick my brain about entrepreneurship—its ups and downs. I strongly encouraged him to strike out on his own. I could tell that he had the wherewithal to make it work. About 18 months ago he left his job and started a company called Skilled Hands on Demand.

He was at my house on a Saturday just as I was starting this chapter. I am writing this in the throes of COVID-19 (April 2020). I asked him how his business was faring, and he excitedly answered, "Booming." He said he does so many different things that there is always a need for his services. He was at my house to do the spring tune-up on the air conditioning system and change the air filters. He told me that I was his fourth call of the day. It was two o'clock in the afternoon. When he left my house, he was going to mount another television.

The conversation turned to his previous employer. He said that he was so glad that he had left because he had been passed over for two promotions. The first time, he was told that he was so good at his current role that they really needed to keep him in that position. He said that they promoted a white man with less experience. The next time, he was told that he had sold too many of a particular service. He is still baffled by that one.

As we continued to talk about his business, he said, "I know that I have to be twice as good. I can't mess up because as it is, when I show up, white people and sometimes even Black people are surprised, and I can see that they are skeptical." He said that as a Black man, even though he is only five feet, five inches tall and slightly built, he senses the fear. "I have to spend more time building rapport and disarming their anxiety. It's crazy, but it is worth it. It is still better than working for my previous employer. I have been doing a lot of reading on the psychology of racism, and even though I just want to do a good job and make a good living for my family, I have to deal with the race stuff too. It is an added burden. It is life."

Everybody Loves Bobby

Bobby (not his real name) was a high-ranking Black man in a major corporation. Over the 30 years that he was with the company, he was consistently given the hardest assignments in various manufacturing plants and the fewest resources. He was the documented "turn-around guy." He would be assigned to the lowest-performing unit and was expected to make it profitable within six months to a year. He was so good at it that he received many accolades and external awards for these accomplishments.

When I met Bobby, he was excited about his new role in diversity and inclusion. In the job for just over a year, he approached it as a turn-around opportunity. He boasted about how he had added structure and outcomes for the employee resource groups so that they could clearly show how they added value to the company. Drawing on his manufacturing acumen, he put into place a key performance indicators (KPIs) process. He had a wall in his office for each of the employee resource groups that demonstrated their yearly accomplishments.

Everybody at the company seemed to know, love, and respect Bobby. When you mentioned his name, people would smile and say, He is a great guy.

Bobby decided to retire early because it was obvious that the company was not really serious about diversity and inclusion. He was never able to meet with the CEO to discuss the strategy, and there was little follow-through on the agreed-on objectives. He left the company without receiving the retirement party that was customary (~~micro~~invalidation, as described in chapter 6), burned out and disappointed that his accomplishments were unrecognized. He said he felt a heavy burden every day coming into work, knowing that he would have to work twice as hard for any little "win" to move the diversity agenda. When I asked him how he is doing now as an independent consultant in manufacturing operations, he said "fantastic"—a great burden had been lifted from him.

I share Ryon's and Bobby's stories because we do not hear much about the Ryons and the Bobbys of the world. They are invisible. The everyday Black men who are working overtime hard, striving, married with children, just trying to build a better life. More often than not, the picture that is painted of the Black man in America has not changed much since slavery—that of a scary, threatening, criminal, less-than-human menace to society.

Nice, Scary, Hostile, Deviant?

Terrence Harewood, a friend and consultant to The Winters Group, is a college professor. He recounted a story about himself and a Black male colleague on their first day in their doctoral program. They were the only two Black men in the program. On the first day, students were asked to introduce themselves. At a break, two white women came up to them and said, "We were just talking about you two. You are *so* nice." Terrence said that all he and the other Black student did was say their names and where they were from. "How could they possibly know from these brief introductions whether or not we were 'nice'?" Terrence said he felt that was code for, "We do not expect Black men to be nice. You are not scary like our image of Black men." He said he feels the burden all the time of thinking about, "Am I being nice enough so they will not see my over six-foot frame and dark skin as a threat? I am tired of having to worry about if I am nice enough. Whose discomfort is at stake to ensure that they are comfortable?" While, on the surface, "nice" is a positive description, it can be said in ways that imply, You are different—not the scary, angry Black man. It is a ~~micro~~insult, as described in chapter 6.

Even a Black Santa Claus can be scary to white people. I was in a CVS near the Christmas holidays in 2019. I walked in and saw two five-foot Santa Clauses on display, one white and one Black. As I passed them, I said to myself, "How inclusive." I was happy to see the diversity and acknowledgment that Santa could actually be a person of color. After picking up a prescription, I was leaving the store, passing the Santas again, and a white couple was entering. I overheard the woman say, "Oh, that Black Santa Claus is so scary." I left thinking, If she thinks a statue of a Black Santa is scary, what must she think about live Black men? The only difference between the white and Black Santa was the color of the paint used for their faces.

While there are many characterizations of Black men as scary, monstrous types, scholars often point to D. W. Griffith's highly successful yet very controversial 1915 silent film, *The Birth of a Nation*,[3] which sadistically portrays Black men as unintelligent, lazy, and sexually aggressive, especially toward white women. It provides a justification for the KKK to protect the world from dangerous Black men. Protests from civil rights groups calling for discontinuation of its showing were ignored, and the film in fact led to increased violence against Blacks. My son, Joseph Winters, professor of religious studies at Duke University, asserts in his book, *Hope Draped in Black: Race, Melancholy, and the Agony of Progress*,[4] that the portrayals of Black men and women on the big screen often still perpetuate negative stereotypes today. In the last chapter, I mentioned the critique that Halle Berry's role in *Monster's Ball* perpetuated the hypersexualized Black woman stereotype. Winters says that Denzel Washington's portrayal in *Training Day* of a rogue police detective, for which he won the Oscar for Best Actor in 2002, amplified the "fears and anxieties associated with the deviant Black male body."[5] Some also argued that it was because he played this stereotypical role that he won the top Oscar honor and that there were earlier roles that were even more worthy, such as his portrayal of Malcom X, for which he was nominated for Best Actor in 1993.

Black men are not a monolith. However, similar to Black women, Black men share experiences that are unique to them as a group based on their identifiable characteristics, skin color and gender. While men are not usually identified as a stigmatized group like women, Black men, by and large, do not enjoy the power and privilege afforded white men based on their group membership as "men." For example, research shows that white men often benefit from exhibiting stereotypically "masculine" behavior in the workplace. However, men of color are more likely to be penalized for the same behaviors. For example, Latinos, especially those of Mexican national origin, endure stereotypes in some settings that describe them as emotional and "macho" with negative connotations. They also may be stereotyped as too aggressive and too dominant. Black men are often stereotyped as aggressive and hostile and associated with violence and street crime.[6]

Tall, Dark, and Handsome?

Studies show that tall men enjoy privileges that short men do not.[7] For example, women find tall men more attractive. Tall men are more likely to succeed in business. Sixty percent of CEOs are over six feet tall, while only 15 percent of the male population is over six feet. Tall men make more money than short men. For every additional inch of height, men make on average $800 more per year. (Note: The median income of a Black man in 2017 was $41,347, compared with $60,388 for white men.)

However, these favorable perceptions do not hold true for Black men. The taller the Black man, the more threatening he is perceived to be. Based on research conducted by psychologists from the University of North Carolina at Chapel Hill, for every one white man over six feet four stopped by the police, 6.2 Black men were stopped. In another study, where 318 participants were asked to look at photographs of 16 young men, half white and half Black, the taller the white subjects, the more likely they were rated as competent and nonthreatening. The opposite was true for the Black subjects. They were rated as incompetent and threatening.[8] There is an interesting caveat, however. When "threat" is removed from the equation, tall black men, like tall white men, project the same aura of competence. The researchers concluded that a Black male business executive may be positively perceived at a board meeting—and then negatively stereotyped when he takes off his suit and goes for a run.

There are numerous stories of professional Black men who say that even if they are going into the office on a weekend, they dress in business attire for fear of being questioned by security. Even on "casual Fridays," Black men often are still very mindful of how their "look" may trigger negative stereotypes and are more apt to dress more formally—and definitely not wear a hoodie. Hillary Clinton declared in a campaign speech in 2015 that even "open-minded white people" are sometimes afraid of hoodie-wearing Black men. Black men often work hard to avoid stereotype threats. This extra emotional labor of constantly wondering whether you look threatening is fatiguing.

Two Black men, Andre Wright and Jason Sole, started the Humanize My Hoodie movement (figure 7.1) as a part of Born Leaders United to destigmatize clothing trends associated with BIPOC.[9] The movement includes a book, *Humanize My Hoodie*, allyship workshops, and a clothing line. "We seek to create a world in which our fashion isn't probable cause for us to be slain in the streets," the founders say on their website. They claim that wearing their hoodie has had a positive impact on reversing the negative stereotype.

Figure 7.1. Humanize My Hoodie
Source: Used with permission of Born Leaders United.[10]

While Black women may consider more melanin to be a desirable trait for Black men, in general, light skin color is perceived as better than, more desirable, and less threatening than dark skin. A University of Georgia study with 240 subjects found that a light-skinned Black man with a bachelor's degree was more likely to be hired than a dark-skinned Black man with an MBA.[11] University of San Francisco researchers conducted a study that revealed that educated Black men are remembered by subjects as having lighter skin. The results indicated that participants who were shown the word "educated" had more memory errors and often chose the photos with a lighter-skinned Black man when asked to recall the face they originally saw with darker skin.[12]

Based on a statistical study of the effects of skin tone on wages conducted in 2018 by researchers from several universities, the authors concluded that taller males with darker skin are paid less. As a matter of fact, education made the disparity worse. Dark-skinned college-educated men had even lower earnings compared with individuals with lighter skin. For every one-unit increase in the darkness of skin tone (on a 10-point scale with zero being the lightest and 10 being the darkest), annual real wages decline by $463.88.[13] As stated earlier, height penalizes Black men's salary, and when you add the decrease based on skin tone, it is a double whammy. In this study, skin tone did not affect Black women's salaries.

On Guard

Negative stereotypes put Black men on guard in the workplace. At least 25 percent of men of color report being on guard in the workplace.[14] Black men and women often resort to code switching, adjusting their style of speech, appearance, behavior, and expression in ways that will optimize the comfort of the dominant group in the workplace (white people). Black men, especially tall ones, are often assumed to have prowess in sports. "You must be good at basketball" is a statement my son, Joe, often heard because of his six-foot-four frame. He was a much better scholar than he was an athlete (~~micro~~invalidation). The stereotypes of "the good" Black men as entertainers, sports figures, or musicians and not business leaders or scholars cause cognitive dissonance for many whites and frustration and fatigue for Black men.

Whether educated or not, Black men continue to conjure up images of the "boogeyman," and it is detrimental to their health, income, safety, and overall well-being. Living as a Black man in America is a scary proposition. It is fatiguing.

Tokenized and Silenced

Black men, like Black women, are tokenized in many of the same ways. They are selected to be a part of a diversity committee and expected to be the voice of all Black men in the organization. Or their Black presence is desired, but their voices are not welcome. I participated in a "fireside chat" recently with the CEO of a very large company in response to the Black Lives Matter protests of 2020. The virtual event was broadcast to all employees. A high-ranking Black man at the company was also invited. The virtual session was conducted by the three of us. As I understood the assignment, it was to be a one-hour question-and-answer session with me bringing the outside expertise and the Black man providing an internal perspective. I was dismayed that the process consisted of the CEO and the Black executives taking turns asking me questions for the whole hour. The Black executive's only role was to query me. I so badly wanted to ask him to share his thoughts, and in hindsight I wish I had. It was definitely not clear to me in our prep call several days before the event that this was the only role the Black executive would play. I imagine he felt invalidated and even invisible.

An "Us or Them" Existence

The Winters Group uses a tool called the Intercultural Development Inventory[15] (IDI) to access cultural competence. It is a psychometric instrument that measures one's worldview toward difference. The first two orientations (denial and polarization) are considered monocultural worldviews, where your perspectives are shaped only by your experiences. The model proposes that at these two stages, you have a more simplistic, judgmental worldview. The next orientation is minimization, a worldview that focuses on similarities (e.g., color blind, all lives matter). The last two orientations are acceptance and adaptation. At acceptance, one has a more complex understanding of differences and is able to discern them in a nonjudgmental way. Adaptation is the ability to not only discern differences but also effectively navigate them. I more often find Black men at polarization on the continuum, representing a judgmental "us and them" worldview. When I share these results, they are usually not surprised. Responses often go something like this: "I do see the world as an 'us and them.' I have to constantly watch out for 'them' as a Black man because I know that I am hated, seen as dangerous and someone to be feared." A vice president of a large corporation said, "We are confronted with daily situations that make you see the world as us and them. I guess to move along this continuum, I have to let go of the cuts and bruises that I have had. No matter how much I want the world to be different, it is not. It is a matter of survival, and I do not know how else to see the world. This is my reality."

I Can't Breathe

While Eric Garner and George Floyd literally could not breathe and tragically lost their lives, this sentiment can be figuratively applied to many Black men in America. If we use "I can't breathe" as a metaphor for anxiety, fear, and lack of true freedom, many Black men cannot breathe.

As mentioned in chapter 4, NewsOne reported in June of this year that 83 Black men and boys have been killed by police.[16]

Black people are three times more likely to be killed by police. Philando Castile was shot and killed after being pulled over for a routine stop with his girlfriend and toddler in the car; Trayvon Martin, 14, was killed while walking home from the store after buying Skittles; Tamir Rice was 12 when he was shot and killed by a police officer, seconds after he came on the scene. Rice was playing with a toy gun. In each of these cases, the police officers were acquitted. According to Mapping Police Violence, 99 percent of killings by police from 2013 to 2019 have not resulted in the officers being charged with a crime.[17]

Black people, and Black men in particular, are more likely to be stopped by police. Based on a Stanford University study of 93 million traffic stops from 21 states between 2001 and 2017, Black motorists were 20 percent more likely to be stopped by police.[18]

Several years ago I was conducting a session at a country club in suburban Ohio. One of the participants, a Black male, was late for the session. It was not until the break that he shared with me that he had been stopped by the police for no apparent reason. They asked him where he was going and intimated that they do not usually see people like him in that area driving an expensive car. He told me that he was having trouble concentrating on the session because he was still shaken and angry about the experience. As it was a diversity training session, I asked him whether he wanted to share the experience with the group. He declined because he did not want to "call attention to himself" and he doubted that most would understand anyway.

Blame a Black Man Syndrome

As pointed out in chapter 3, Black men are incarcerated at three times their representation in the population. I noted that the spike in the number of incarcerations happened during the 1980s as a result of Ronald Reagan's War on Drugs initiative, which attached inordinately long sentences to drug offenses.

I also pointed out that Black men are the largest group to be exonerated for being wrongly accused of crimes that they did not commit, largely because of what can be called "blame a Black man" syndrome. This refers to white people blaming Black men for crimes they committed themselves or making false accusations that are not investigated by law enforcement because they are so "believable" in light of entrenched stereotypes of Black men as criminals.

One of the most famous instances of this was when Susan Smith killed her two young children but blamed it on some imaginary Black man and immediately police started an all-out search for "him." Amanda Knox blamed a Black man when she was accused of killing her roommate in Italy. It left the falsely accused man, Diya "Patrick" Lumumba, a local business owner, bankrupt. There is a pattern, based on negative biases about Black men and positive ones about white women, that pushes law enforcement to aggressively pursue the alleged perpetrator. As mentioned in the preface, Amy Cooper accused a Black birdwatcher (Christian Cooper—not related) in Central Park of threatening her and her dog because he requested that she follow the park's leash regulations. In video recorded by Christian Cooper, Amy Cooper pretends to be in imminent danger, calling 911 and screaming for the police to hurry because an African American man is threatening her.

It feeds the stereotype from *The Birth of a Nation* and other portrayals that Black men are violent and obsessed with white women, necessitating extra protection for them from Black men.

Mass Incarceration

As discussed in chapter 3, mass incarceration is a serious social issue in this country that disproportionately affects Black and Brown people and Black men in particular. Black men account for 6 percent of the population; however, 15 percent of Black men in the United States have been to prison, compared with 6 percent of all adult men, and social scientists predict that one in three Black men will face prison time during their lifetime. As stated earlier, Black people also account for 47 percent of the exonerations.

Black men are more likely to be incarcerated on drug charges, and white men are more likely to be sent to rehabilitation. Eighty percent of the incarcerated in federal prisons for drug offenses are Black.[19] Black people are no more likely to use drugs than white people. Black men get longer sentences and have higher rates of recidivism because of entrenched systems that make it difficult to reenter society.

In a report in 2018 to the United Nations from the Sentencing Project on the racial disparities in the US criminal justice system, recommendations to the UN special rapporteur included ending the War on Drugs to reduce the number of low-level drug offenders prosecuted in federal court; eliminating mandatory minimum sentences; not retaining defendants pretrial because they cannot afford bail if they do not pose a safety or flight risk; requiring racial impact statements for proposed sentencing policies; and requiring implicit bias training at every level of the criminal justice system, among others.[20] I do not think that any of these recommendations has gained traction.

Mass incarceration of Black men, in part, explains why Black people are much less likely to be married. In 2016 in the United

States, 29 percent of Black people were married, compared with 48 percent of all Americans.[21] There is a shortage of eligible Black men. Interestingly, until the 1960s Black and white rates of marriage were essentially the same, and then there was steep widening of the gap that persists today. It was during this time that the rates of mass incarceration began to increase sharply for Black men. Incarceration rates are more than 500 percent higher than they were 40 years ago. Another factor contributing to lower marriage rates is job instability for Black men. According to a study conducted by the Census Bureau and National Bureau of Economic Research, Black men fare worse economically than white men even if they are raised in households with similar incomes and educated similarly. A Black boy brought up in a wealthy family is as likely to become poor in adulthood as he is to remain prosperous.[22] Lower marriage rates negatively affect chances for economic stability, as highlighted in chapter 3.

Mass incarceration is also a public health issue. During the COVID-19 outbreak in 2020, the horrors of the prison system were once again illuminated. Overcrowding and poor sanitation put prisoners at higher risk. Many Black men in prison are already health compromised. Reports of guards and prisoners testing positive for COVID-19 were especially sobering since quarantines are nearly impossible among incarcerated populations. To address this, some jurisdictions released prisoners. In doing so, it was also re-uncovered that many Black men were in prison for minor offenses and had sentences disproportionately longer than their white counterparts for the same offense.[23]

Mass incarceration is a well-entrenched system to perpetuate structural racism. It affects every aspect of one's life from socioeconomics to voting, employment, and personal relationships. It is a form of genocide.

Man Up with Barber Shop Therapy and Healing for Black Men

I pointed out in chapter 4 that the life expectancy of Black men is the lowest of every group—almost a decade lower than that of white women. I also shared how Black men are more likely than other segments of the population to have undiagnosed or poorly managed chronic conditions (e.g., diabetes, cancers, heart disease). For example, prostate cancer is the most common illness among men, and Black men are more likely to get it and twice as likely to succumb to it. Additionally, Black men are the only demographic group for which homicide is one of the top five causes of death.[24]

Black men are also more likely to delay seeking medical care. There are various reasons for not seeking care, including lack of access. Black men are more likely to live in poverty than their white counterparts and less likely to have health insurance. Even with a job, more Black men, like Black women, are employed in industries that do not offer health insurance.

Lack of trust is also a significant factor in Black men not seeking care. I highlighted the issue of trust in chapter 4, which is tied to the widespread experimentation on Black people without our approval throughout history. The most famous involving Black men is perhaps the Tuskegee syphilis study. A study in *Harvard Business Review* in 2018 reported that Black men were more likely to seek treatment when the physician was also Black because of a greater level of trust.[25]

Machoism is also a factor. Research shows that Black men are the least likely to seek out mental health support because of the "tough guy" syndrome. The Michigan-based Man Up Man Down research program studies the physical and emotional health of Black men. Based on focus group research in six cities from 2010 to 2018, the researchers found some consistent themes when they asked what it means to be a "real man," including being tough and self-sufficient, and they found that many Black men embrace the tough-guy syndrome as a source of self-esteem and self-respect. The researchers assert that the syndrome contributes to Black men being the least likely to seek mental health services—almost half as likely as white men.[26]

Black men often receive "counseling" from their barbers, known as "barbershop therapy." They have found that this is a safe, nonjudgmental, trusting environment where they are able to unload their burdens. The Confess Project, a nonprofit based in Little Rock, Arkansas, is training barbers to be front-line counselors for clients who are depressed or traumatized. The initiative is also now in Kentucky, Tennessee, South Carolina, Georgia, and Louisiana. Its website asks, "Ever been told to 'man up' when all you wanted to do is cry? Wished there was someone to talk to who understood where you were coming from? Had a moment when all the -isms in life were too much to bear? We've been there."[27]

Jeff Johnson, who had a career as a journalist, producer, and TV host, now runs Men Thrive,[28] a nonprofit that provides "a community that is curated to proclaim the generational toxic stress, depression, and anxiety standing in the way of us [Black men] living our best lives as something that must end." Men Thrive debunks the narrative that Black men must hide their feelings, be tough, and "fix their faces" (don't show emotion). Johnson's organization seeks to reprogram the brain with self-mastery tools and positive affirmations in support of Black men "showing up whole, operating with joy, and living with power."

Show Me Some Respect

What does it mean today to be a Black man in the United States? Ralph Ellison's characterization of his protagonist as "invisible" is an apt metaphor for the historical and current social realities for many Black boys and men. Ellison's story ends with the "invisible man" being chased by police during a riot in Harlem and falling into a manhole in the middle of the street. The police put the cover of the manhole back in place, trapping the man in the hole. "I'm an invisible man and it placed me in a hole—or showed me the hole I was in, if you will—and I reluctantly accepted the fact,"[29] writes Ellison. Many Black men today can relate to the character's experience of feeling trapped in a hole and irrelevant. The Winters Group conducted healing sessions with Black employees from several companies at the height of the Black Lives Matter protests in 2020. Black men used words like "invisible," "ignored," "isolated," "unheard," "threatening," "misunderstood," "muzzled," and "unsafe" to describe their existence in the workplace.

They carry the weight of invisibleness with many different and sometimes destructive responses. Black men have a number of different personas, including nurturing father figure; supportive partner; strong, don't-show-emotion macho man; laid back; (nothing bothers me); a hard, mean outward vibe (I'll kick your ass if you mess with me). Behind these different personas hide deep wounds from intergenerational denigration. As a result of centuries of mistreatment and being characterized as subhuman, sexually aggressive, threatening, and lazy, for some, these perceptions have been internalized and take many different forms of outward behaviors on the scale from passivity to aggression—from a carefree, happy demeanor to rage. It is a part of the post-traumatic slave syndrome that Joy DeGruy describes.[30]

The Man Up Man Down research also found that Black men said being a real man included providing for your family, achieving the respect of others, and attaining financial success. Because Black men are more likely not to be able to provide for their families as a result of discriminatory workplace practices, they cannot achieve financial success, which means they also will not achieve the respect of others. This leads to depression, anger, and rage, which, as I pointed out earlier, more often than not goes untreated.

Black men want to be respected. For the most part they get little real respect in the white world and therefore yearn for it and even demand it from their own community. The term "diss," which has been appropriated by most of popular culture, originated in the Black community to mean disrespect, and you should not disrespect a Black man or be ready to suffer a range of consequences, as described earlier. This deep-seated quest for respect can manifest too often in patriarchy and turning to an alternate (illegal by dominant standards) economy for income.

Patriarchy, Sexism, Misogyny, and Abuse

Patriarchy shows up in Black culture in explicit and subtle ways. One manifestation is in the church. In some Black churches, women are not allowed to be full-fledged clergy, and in some cases they are not even allowed to sit in the pulpit. I remember a number of years ago being baffled when I was asked to be the Women's Day speaker at a church but was told that I would not be able to sit in the pulpit. I also notice how Black men often savor the prestige of being a trustee or a steward or on the deacon board. If they have a lay leadership role, they take it very seriously. The church is one of perhaps only a few places where they can get respect and also utilize talents that may be underutilized in the corporate world. Patriarchy and sexism are often defended by narrow interpretations of the Bible.

Misogynist messages are common in the hip-hop music world. Consider the case brought against rap group 2 Live Crew in 1990. They were arrested on obscenity charges for sexually explicit lyrics that denigrated Black women in their song "Nasty as You Wanna Be." The case was later dismissed, but the controversy remains as to whether these types of lyrics in hip-hop fuel the "rape culture" and sexual violence against Black women. Henry Louis Gates Jr., a prominent Black historian at Harvard University, argued that 2 Live Crew was intending to exaggerate stereotypes about Black men and women to show how ridiculous they are and push white society's buttons. Kimberlé Crenshaw weighed in, opposing Gates and arguing that these harmful images are still too real in the minds of many white people and that young people who listen to these messages may embody them.[31]

When Kobe Bryant died tragically in 2020, Snoop Dogg denigrated Gayle King publicly, using misogynist language, for bringing up the 2003 rape charges against Bryant in an interview with Lisa Leslie. He later apologized, but it brings up the complex relationship between Black men and women that dates back to slavery, when families were ripped apart. The slavery-inspired stereotypes of Black women have been internalized by some Black men.

As I pointed out in chapter 6, Black women are much more likely to face domestic violence at the hands of their partners. I also mentioned that they are more likely to "stand by their man," even though they are three times more likely to die from domestic or intimate partner violence than white women.[32] While I certainly would never condone or make excuses for this behavior, I assert that the reasons for these egregious actions are complex. I am only trying to explain that when we simply judge the behavior without exploring the root cause and the role that white supremacy plays, we may draw erroneous conclusions. As I said earlier, Black men want respect, such as that derived from the ability to provide for one's family. With unemployment rates for Black men at twice the rate of white men since 1960, it becomes an affront to one's manhood, and those who are not able to handle the stress may turn to violence. Black women also have their own challenges, as pointed out in chapter 6, and a couple trying to navigate the realities of racism may encounter relationship problems. This is one of the reasons for higher divorce rates[33] and fewer marriages among Black people.

SUMMARY

Black men need and deserve respect. They do not want to be viewed as scary and threatening. They do not want to have to fear for their lives. They want to be able to reach their full potential without the extraordinary burden of living in a white supremacist, racist society.

Black men are fatigued by trying to play by rules that do not work for them or are changed when it looks as if they may support them.

There are many groups around the country that continue to work on the unique issues that Black men face, such as the YMCA, Boys and Girls Clubs, 100 Black Men, Black fraternities, churches, and many others. We Dream a World: The 2025 Vision for Black Men and Boys is a project of the Twenty-First Century Foundation that lays out a comprehensive agenda for reform in five key areas: education, fatherhood and families, employment and wealth, health, and criminal justice.

We have to continue to shine a light on the enormous life obstacles that structural racism and negative stereotyping present for Black men. It will take collective responsibility,[34] which has also been referred to as collective guilt, a social justice concept that individuals are responsible for other people's actions by tolerating, ignoring, or harboring them without actively collaborating in them. From collective responsibility must come collection action.

A major first step is to reframe our equity and justice work on behalf of Black men to focus on asset rather than deficit thinking and actions. What are the positive aspects of Black manhood? Focus on the unique contributions throughout history to build strong, positive self-concepts. Disrupt negative narratives in the media by holding the media accountable for more balanced reporting of Black men. As I mentioned in chapter 3, the media disproportionately uses negative portrayals of Black men which is disturbing and fatiguing.

It is easier to build strong children than to repair broken men.

—Frederick Douglass, American social reformer, abolitionist, orator, writer, and statesman

EIGHT

Out of the Mouths of Babes: Black Children's Fatigue

Joe

My son Joe—yes, the same one mentioned throughout the book, the associate professor of religion at Duke University and the Harvard, Duke, and Princeton graduate—was quite a handful between the ages of two and nine. I was a working mother, so both he and his sister, Mareisha, were in day care and then after-school care. Joe was an especially difficult toddler and young child. He threw his share of tantrums and then some. Popular parenting tools like the time-out chair did not work at all for Joe. He was sent home from the day care center several times for "aggression," fighting, and otherwise unacceptable behavior. (We learned later that allergies may have accounted for some of this behavior.) We tried Montessori school, where he lasted about three weeks. The teacher said that he did not string beads or march the Montessori way. (I thought the whole idea of

Montessori education was that you were free to explore your own way.) Joe was always big for his age. By six months old, he was in the ninety-ninth percentile for weight and height. He was over six feet by the time he was 12. We sought the advice of a child psychologist who basically said that, based on her testing, he was of at least average intelligence. He was just "wired" differently. I am not sure that we learned specific strategies to help Joe from her.

Even with the behavioral issues, Joe has always had a huge heart. One day when he was three years old, I thought he was playing close to home, but I did not see him in the yard. He rode his big wheel to the next-door neighbors', knocked on the door, and said, "Hi, I just came over to see how everybody is doing. You all OK?" The neighbors and I had the biggest laugh. When he was nine years old (1986), he woke up crying one morning because he was concerned that everybody in the whole world would die of AIDS. Still today his caring spirit is what his friends and colleagues admire. At his dissertation defense at Princeton, Cornel West, one of Joe's advisers, said of his protégé, "Joe does not only possess one of the finest minds that I have encountered, he is one of the finest people I have ever known."

Joe went to predominantly white schools and he was often the only Black boy in his class and the tallest. Up until fourth grade, he continued to have various behavioral issues at school. His dad and I were frequently in meetings with teachers. In fourth grade, his white male teacher transformed our perception of Joe from a difficult child of average intelligence to a brilliant one. He said, "I think the only thing wrong with Joe is that he is brilliant and has not been challenged." Almost immediately Joe's grades started to improve, largely, I think, because his self-concept improved. Fast-forward to high school, Joe graduated as valedictorian of his all-male Jesuit school, having attained straight As, and was awarded a four-year full academic scholarship to Harvard.

If Joe had not had a teacher in fourth grade who was able to see beyond the prevailing stereotypes of Black boys (less intelligent, aggressive) and see his potential, Joe's life story may have been very different. Even we, as parents, were buying into the deficit narrative about Joe. I just wanted Joe to comply and to stop causing trouble. I did not thoroughly consider the role that implicit bias played in his earlier teachers' assessments. I did not probe enough with Joe as to his day-to-day school experiences that may have contributed to his behavior. I do know that it was frustrating and fatiguing for us as parents and certainly for Joe, coming of age as a Black boy in the 1980s in America.

What about all the Black children who do not have a fourth-grade teacher like Joe's? What about all the brilliant minds that are being lost because they are being stereotyped as less than—not capable?

Mareisha

Joe's sister, Mareisha, did not have any significant issues until third grade. On a report card, she was labeled "lazy." Mareisha was shy as a child, an introvert, but lazy did not seem to fit. When we sought clarification, the teacher told us that Mareisha often put her head down on the desk during music. When we asked Mareisha, she told us that the teacher would come close to her with instruments such as tambourines or maracas and wanted the students to show that they were getting into the rhythm. Mareisha did not like attention on her, so she put her head down and essentially recoiled. Rather than attempt to understand Mareisha's behavior, the teacher judged her based on her interpretation of what putting your head on the desk meant. "Lazy" is a particularly triggering depiction because it is an entrenched stereotype about Black people and not one that we wanted to be a part of Mareisha's record. After much cajoling, the teacher deleted the term "lazy." It was fatiguing.

I share this story because I know that there are many Black parents who are extra vigilant in ensuring that their children are not stereotyped and labeled. The extra emotional toll is fatiguing.

Young, Gifted, and Black

One of The Winters Group's principal strategists, Valda Valbrun, a K–12 educator, laments that children of color often do not feel good about themselves because of the limitations that school systems put on them and the inequities in resource allocation that I mentioned in chapter 3. Valda has worked in several districts as a teacher, principal, and head of teacher development and sees the vast inequities that disproportionately affect Black children. "White teachers and administrations have deep-seated perceptions that Black kids are just incapable of achieving. They pity them and set low expectations." Research shows that Black and Latino students are least likely to be recommended for honors or advanced placement classes.[1] Black and Latino students represent 38 percent of students in schools that offer AP courses, but only 29 percent of students enrolled in at least one AP course. Black and Latino students also have less access to gifted and talented education programs than white students.

According to the Office of Civil Rights, Black students—and, in particular, Black boys—were two to three times more likely to be enrolled in special education classes than their nonblack peers.

Black students without disabilities are more than three times as likely as their white peers without disabilities to be expelled or suspended. Although Black students represent 15 percent of students in the Office of Civil Rights database, they make up 35 percent of students suspended once, 44 percent of those suspended more than once, and 36 percent of students expelled. Further, over 50 percent of students who were involved in school-related arrests or referred to law enforcement are Hispanic or Black.[2] As mentioned in chapter 3, Black children represent 19 percent of the nation's preschool population yet 47 percent of those receiving more than one out-of-school suspension. In contrast, white students represent 41 percent of preschool enrollment but only 28 percent of those receiving more than one out-of-school suspension. As a result, Black students spend less time in the classroom, further affected their access to a quality education.

Over 80 percent of K–12 public teachers are white, while less than half of the students are white.[3]

Research shows that white teachers often pity and underchallenge Black children. They see them in a deficit framework, not capable of meeting, let alone exceeding, standards. Black students with Black teachers are three times more likely to be recommended for gifted programs. When Black and white teachers evaluate the same Black student, white teachers are 12 percent less likely to predict that the student will finish high school and 30 percent less likely to predict that the student will graduate from college.[4]

Children Know

My daughter-in-law, Kamilah Legette, a research associate at the University of North Carolina at Chapel Hill, studies the impact of bias on students of color. Her research[5] reveals that children know when their teachers perceive them to be deficient. Children answered her queries with comments like the following:

- "I mean just because they think they can just look at you and say 'Oh, you're a bad child,' but they actually don't even know you, so that's just what they think before they actually get to know you, but then when they get to know you, their opinions would change and they would think, and then they'll know that you're nice, you're not a bad child."
- "They didn't really think that I had the answer. I was raising my hand to say something, but like the teachers kept calling on white people, not me. But I keep trying. It can be kinda hard, because I feel like my teachers don't like me or think I know things."
- "It's just, I can't really explain it to you, but sometimes it's like I can tell at first they think I'm going to be a certain way and then they find out I'm different."

It is fatiguing and psychologically damaging for children who are eager to learn to experience these biases, intentional or not. These situations can lead to internalized oppression that can follow the child through adulthood.

For my son, Joe, once he was told that he was smart and capable, he started to perform that way. This is called efficacy. I met Jeff Howard, a Harvard-trained psychologist, in the early 1990s. His organization, the Efficacy Institute,[6] works with school administrators to advance the belief that there is nothing wrong with the kids. They can all succeed if they have the right tools and supports. Efficacy is the judgment one makes about one's own ability to achieve. If teachers send messages, either explicit or implicit, that they do not expect the students to succeed, it becomes a self-fulfilling prophecy.

Compounding the racism caused by harmful stereotypes, as pointed out in chapter 3, schools that educate Black and Brown children are underfunded and, in general, underresourced. The coronavirus outbreak again shed light on the digital divide as one of many problems. Students were forced to learn from home and, disproportionately, students of color did not have access to the internet.[7] What is so fatiguing is that this inequity was not new. Why had it not been effectively addressed before the pandemic?

Out of the Mouths of Babes

Internalized oppression starts in preschool. The famous black doll experiment[8] first conducted by psychologists Kenneth and Mamie Clark in the 1940s and repeated several times since is evidence that Black children often have a negative self-image. In the experiment, researchers show Black children ages four to seven several dolls, some white and some black, and ask the children a series of questions about them, including which one is pretty, which one is smart, and which one is good or bad. Ninety-nine percent of the time, the children pick the white doll for the positive attributes and the black doll when the label is negative. When the interviewer asks the children why the white doll is better, some say that it is because it is white. Others will say that it is because it has blue eyes or because it is pretty. The most telling aspect of the experiment is the last question—Which doll looks like you?—in response to which the children point to the black doll. It is very fatiguing that the results have not changed since the 1940s. Then is now.

As mentioned in chapter 1, research demonstrates that babies as young as nine months old show preference for their own race.[9] Researchers do not conclude that this is racism, but it demonstrates that we do notice color early in life.

Childhood Interrupted

Black children often "grow up too fast" because of their social circumstances and stereotypes about their innocence. They experience the effects of structural racism based on where they live, where and what they learn, their economic means (what they have), and their legal means (how their rights are executed).

In 2018, 32 percent of Black children were living in poverty[10] and 65 percent of Black children were living in single-parent households versus 24 percent for white children.[11] As a result, older children may have to carry out more household duties at young ages and be expected to care for younger children while their mother works. These circumstances often lead to chronic absenteeism from school, poor nutrition, and more health challenges, as described later in this chapter.

Black children are perceived to be older and less innocent, regardless of social standing, something known as adultification bias. Studies show that Black boys as young as 10 are viewed as older and therefore more responsible for their actions, whereas white boys of the same age are presumed innocent. We, as Black people, can feed into that narrative by using names like "little man" as terms of endearment. We also often feed into the stereotype that boys should not cry as it is a sign of weakness.

Young Black boys are often taught how to withhold and withdraw to avoid provoking the fear or ire of those around them.[12] As I mentioned, my son, Joe, was tall for his age from the time he was a toddler. He was often told in day care to be careful because he could hurt the other children because of his size. Regarding Black girls, compared with white girls of the same age, they are seen as needing less support and nurturing and as knowing more about adult topics, including sex.[13]

The Talk

Many Black parents have "the talk" with their children. The talk is about racism and police brutality against Blacks. Parents know that there is a high likelihood that at some point during their adolescence, their children will encounter racism in the form of an undeserved encounter with the police. The talk goes something like this: "As Black people, we continue to be subjected to unfair treatment based on the color of our skin, especially from law enforcement. If you are stopped, even if there seems to be no reason for it and you think you are right, just follow their

Black target
Source: The Winters Group, Inc. Art by Krystle Nicholas.

instructions. Keep your hands in sight—on the steering wheel or up in the air. Do not make a move without their permission, and when you do, tell them exactly what you are doing—for example, reaching into the glove box for the registration. Only answer the questions directly, with no additional commentary. If you are taken into custody, immediately call me and I will take it from there. Your job is to live." Ta-Nehisi Coates wrote a book in the form of a letter to his teenage son. It's titled *Between the World and Me*,[14] and it draws on history as well as personal experience to discuss the different forms of violence against young Blacks. Adolescent psychiatrist Adrienne Clark says "the talk" should start as early as age six with age-appropriate language. At this age she recommends a book called *Something Happened in Our Town: A Child's Story about Racial Injustice.*[15]

The emotional burden this necessity puts on children and parents is fatiguing.

Racism Makes Children Sick Too

Chapter 4 highlights the deep-seated and systemic nature of racial disparities in health care and outcomes. These disparities start in the womb from maternal exposure to stress manifested by preterm and low birth weights and carry through adulthood as higher incidences of heart disease, diabetes, and depression. As pointed out in chapter 4, the stress generated by early experiences with racism has been proven to create toxic stress.

Black children are exposed to more racial stress by situations at home, poverty, experiences in school, the fear of being racially profiled by police, and the denial of their innocence. Stress leads to actual changes in hormones that cause inflammation in the body, an indicator of chronic disease. Researchers have found that Black children are more prone to toxic stress (trauma). Based on research from the Opportunity Institute, they assert, "'Stress' is a commonplace term for hormonal changes that occur in response to frightening or threatening events or conditions. When severe, these changes are termed 'toxic' stress and can impede children's behavior, cognitive capacity, and emotional and physical health." Events that can engender toxic stress include a parent or close family member being incarcerated; the witnessing of domestic violence; physical or emotional neglect; financial hardships; exposure to external violence; divorce or separation of parents; overt discrimination; and placement in foster care. As has been discussed throughout the book, Black people disproportionately experience all of these stressors, which all can be tied to structural racism.[16]

As pointed out in this chapter and in chapter 4, Black children are more likely to live in poverty, experience environmental racism (be food insecure, live in a food desert, or not have access to clean water), lack access to good-quality health care, suffer from poor nutrition, not get enough sleep, and not receive a good education.

Racism's impact on children's health is vast. It leads to weathering, as pointed out in chapter 4. Youths who experience discrimination early in life face accelerated aging. They are also diagnosed with depression more often. In the University of Georgia study, depression among Black youth was significant at ages 10–15 and 20–29. Chapter 4 points out that Black children die more often from sudden infant death syndrome and are more likely to have asthma, be obese, and attempt suicide in high school due to depression.

The connected systemic issues interrupt Black childhood, affect their academic achievement, and almost guarantee that the cycle will be repeated for the next generation.

SUMMARY

Children are our most precious gift. They deserve the best. Black children deserve the best too if we are to break the cycle of intergenerational fatigue. When children are taught that they are gifted and have unlimited potential, they fulfill that narrative. When they are told that they are less intelligent and older than their years, they also fulfill that narrative.

Marian Wright Edelman, founder of the Children's Defense Fund and activist for children's rights, said, "If we don't stand up for our children, we don't stand for much." We often declare that children are our future. Are only some children our future and others OK to "throw away"? What can we do?

Take a systems approach: Even though there are numerous organizations and efforts working on the issues that I highlight in this chapter, I wonder whether there is enough of a coordinated, collaborative national effort to change the trajectory. I wonder whether we really are changing systems or simply focusing on programmatic solutions. There are initiatives such as Advancing Equity for Women and Girls of Color, which was started with the Obama administration. I do not think it has gotten much traction. A nationwide Boys and Men of Color initiative has taken root in a number of cities based on findings from the My Brother's Keeper task force. Programs often have an objective of changing the children or helping the children cope rather than changing the system, which would mean dismantling policies and practices that perpetuate structural racism. Systems are hard to crack, but that is what it will take. (I realize this is not new news.) Programs tied to larger systems change such as Head Start, a federally funded preschool program, have worked to improve school readiness.

Distribute school resources equitably: As mentioned in chapter 3, schools that educate Black and Brown children are woefully underfunded. Often districts are funded based on an equality (everybody gets the same amount) rather than an equity model (resource allocation is based on need). I think this is an easy fix. It is tangible and quantifiable. Every child should have access to technology—a computer and internet access.

Change the narrative about who Black children are and what they are capable of: Media images need to change. Deficit thinking needs to change. Parents are mainly responsible for this, but teachers play a big role too. We can all play our part in debunking myths and shattering stereotypes. It takes a village.

Fix economic inequities: The rich get richer and the poor get poorer, as the saying goes. The cycle of poverty cannot be broken if we have systems that favor those with higher incomes over those with lower incomes. While I realize this is a complex issue, fraught with politics and different worldviews, it could be fixed if we wanted to do it. Some countries, including many European countries, pay parents when they have children as a means of reducing poverty, something known as a child allowance. Some countries pay poorer parents more (equity model). They get this allowance whether they work or not, a basic difference from the United States' child tax credit.[17]

Provide incentives for larger grocers to operate in Black and Brown communities: Children need access to healthy food. I discussed food deserts in chapter 4. The lack of access to nutritional food leads to poor health outcomes. According to the United States Department of Agriculture (USDA), nearly 30 million people live in food deserts. Family Dollar, Lyft, and Thrive Market are addressing this issue. Family Dollars are often located in low-income areas and have started carrying fresh fruit. Lyft, the ride-sharing app, is providing rides to Washington, DC residents to larger food chains. Thrive Market, an online retailer sells organic foods at 50 percent off retail prices.[18]

Mandate that landlords provide safe, lead-free, clean housing: As mentioned in chapter 6, Black and Brown families are often living in substandard housing. Even though there are policies to prevent this, there is little monitoring and it takes months, if not years, to bring the perpetrators to justice.

Love your children and love somebody else's too: Children need love. They need encouragement. They need hope. They need to know that adults believe in them.

Changing the world for children will change the world for all and lift the burden of Black fatigue.

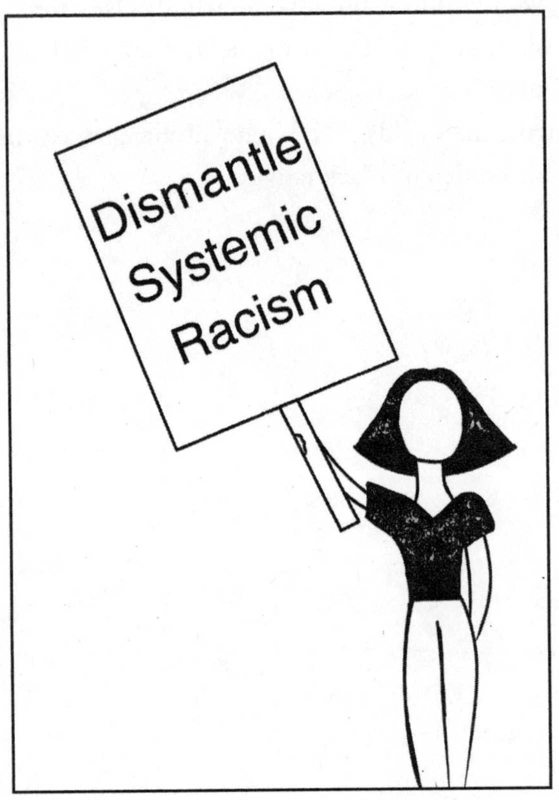

The battle is and always has been a battle for the hearts and minds of white people in this country. The fight against racism is our issue. It's not something that we're called on to help people of color with. We need to become involved with it as if our lives depended on it because really, in truth, they do.

—Ann Braden (1924–2006), white civil rights activist and journalist

NINE

A Clarion Call for Collective Action to Combat Black Fatigue

The Black Lives Matter protests sparked by George Floyd's murder in May 2020 started a new movement for racial justice. Floyd's murder was the boiling point for centuries of injustices that I have highlighted throughout the book.

An opposite of suffering from fatigue is being "indefatigable," meaning relentless, tireless, unwavering, dogged, assiduous, or unstoppable. I think those describers are apt to characterize white supremacist systems. However, Black and white people and non-Black people of color who are allies and power brokers in this new movement to dismantle racism are just as dogged and relentless. The resounding message from the Black Lives Matter protesters after the George Floyd killing was, "We are tired and we want change now."

We do not want more band-aids in the form of programs designed to "fix" Black people. Black people are not the problem.

Racist systems need to be dismantled. Removing confederate statues, eliminating racially stereotyped branding, renaming buildings, and legislating Juneteenth as a national holiday are symbolic but will not necessarily change systems.

We need white people to acknowledge their complicity in perpetuating white supremacy and own their responsibility to dismantle it. White people have been active in combating racism throughout history, such as those who fought to end slavery. William Lloyd Garrison, John Brown, and Harriet Beecher Stowe are a few of the more well-known white abolitionists. Today people like Chris Crass,[1] a white antiracist organizer and author of several books, including *Towards the "Other America": Anti-racist Resources for White People Taking Action for Black Lives Matter*,[2] work to end white supremacy. He was a part of the original group that launched the national network Showing Up for Racial Justice (SURJ).[3] SURJ, with chapters throughout the country, is composed of individuals and groups of white activists who recognize their responsibility in undermining white supremacy. SURJ trains white people how to own their responsibility through active participation in delegitimizing racist institutions. Its programs include training on organizing, the nature of activism, how to hold conversations with skeptics, and understanding the intertwining nature of white supremacy. Many white people joined Black protesters during the Black Lives Matter rebellions in 2020.

What Should White People Do?

1. **Address America's "original sin" of slavery.**[4] While there have been congressional attempts to call for a formal apology for slavery as well as reparations, the bills have never

passed. We should take a page from South Africa's Truth and Reconciliation Commission that assigned accountability for apartheid. An apology is not so much about making the wronged party feel better as it is about accountability. The United States has apologized to other wronged groups, such as the Japanese internees during World War II, and paid reparations. Why does this apparently simple but very meaningful act for Black Americans seem to be too much to fathom?

The wealth gap that I outlined in chapter 3 cannot be corrected with individual responsibility. We cannot catch up through hard work. The intergenerational loss of wealth directly caused by slavery and continued by postslavery racism needs to be corrected with reparations. I believe the US government owes lost wages and damages to the descendants of slaves to begin to level the playing field.[5] Georgetown and Princeton Universities are attempting to rectify the fact that the sale of slaves enhanced their endowments by establishing reparation funds to provide scholarships to descendants of slaves.[6] The apology should be easy, and if there were a real interest in addressing racism, reparations would be understood as a major part of the healing and reconciliation process. Without reparations, the socioeconomic disparities will continue.

There are at least 10 major corporations that profited from the slave trade. These companies should offer reparations by at the very least acknowledging their participation, investing in Black-owned businesses, and ensuring equity in their workforce representation.[7]

2. **Interrogate and change systems instead of adding more programs to fix Black people.** Many companies made

commitments to address racism at the height of the Black Lives Matter movement sparked by George Floyd's death in 2020. They pledged millions of philanthropic dollars to civil rights and social justice organizations, set aggressive representation goals, pledged money to help small Black-owned businesses, declared Juneteenth a holiday, and strengthened their zero-tolerance policies. Is this simply performative activism, just on the surface, meant to increase the organization's social capital or is there a real desire for systemic change?

Too many hurriedly issued these commitments without considering a longer-term, more systemic approach. For many of the Black employees we spoke with during our listening and healing sessions, there was skepticism about the sincerity or the ability of their company to make good on these promises. The commitments were approved by the CEO and developed most often by their inner circle, which is, by and large, white. Perhaps they consulted with their internal diversity leaders, but several told me that was not the case. Perhaps they consulted with one or two external Black leaders. Corporate leaders admitted their sublime ignorance about racial issues. However, in my view, they continued to make decisions about the path forward without the requisite knowledge. A copycat response ensued, with most companies pledging similar actions, almost as if no company wanted to be "one-upped" in the new social justice movement.

What can companies do to change systems? Do not stand on the social justice sidelines.

- Start with the criminal justice system. Support the recommendations to the UN special rapporteur highlighted in chapter 7.

- Get involved in reforming police departments. Take a stand on police brutality. Educate your employees.
- Ensure that all public schools have the resources they need to provide a quality education. Technology companies, ensure that every child in every school district has a computer. Telecommunications companies, eliminate the digital divide.
- Lobby for equitable, not equal, K–12 school funding. School district funding is often determined, in part, by the local tax base.[8]
- Banks, change your practices of refusing a disproportionate number of Black people loans by enacting equitable rather than "equal" requirements. Require that loan officers understand the historical, systemic lack of access to capital that Black people face.
- Buy goods and services from Black-owned businesses.
- Internally, conduct cultural audits to uncover disparate outcomes for Black, Indigenous, and other people of color (BIPOC), disaggregating the results for each identity group (Black, Black women, Black men, etc.). For example, investigate disproportionality in performance ratings and voluntary and involuntary terminations. Conduct a "reverse engineering" process to backtrack and determine where in the system the inequities are occurring. Black people report feeling isolated, ignored, undervalued, and on guard. Hold leaders accountable for creating inclusive cultures that really include everyone. Listen to and incorporate Black people's recommendations. Reevaluate the role of the traditional gatekeepers like those in Legal and HR. These functions often

intentionally or unintentionally minimize or attempt to placate Black people. Develop new ways of thinking about the legal risks associated with more transparency. To authentically address racism, legal risk-aversion tactics may need to be changed.

- Corporate America, discontinue striving to get on lists of "diversity best" this and that based on unspoken "pay to play" criteria. Companies pay out hundreds of thousands of dollars annually to increase the chances of being on the "best company for diversity" list. Reallocate those dollars to improving the internal culture for BIPOC and supporting organizations dedicated to eradicating racism.

3. **Acknowledge white supremacy and become antiracist.** First, if an organization is truly antiracist, it will acknowledge its complicity in perpetuating racist systems.

In chapter 2, I shared the difference between a nonracist and an antiracist, the former being someone who declares that they are not racist and the latter being someone who is actively involved in dismantling racism. Ibram X. Kendi says in his book *How to Be an Antiracist*[9] that when we choose to be antiracist, we are conscious about race and racism and take actions to end racial inequities, such as supporting and voting for policies that create racial equity.

Being antiracist is different for white people and people of color. For white people, being antiracist evolves with their racial identity development.[10] They must acknowledge and understand their privilege, work to change their internalized racism, and interrupt racism when they see it. For people of color, it means recognizing how race and racism have been internalized.

The Ben & Jerry's ice cream brand provides a good example of an organization taking on white supremacy. In a statement made after George Floyd's murder, the company said that Floyd's death was a result of "inhumane police brutality that is perpetuated by a culture of white supremacy. What happened to George Floyd was not the result of a bad apple; it was the predictable consequence of a racist and prejudiced system and culture that has treated Black bodies as the enemy from the beginning."[11] Organizations that are serious about changing systems will need to start using antiracist language and embrace social justice approaches in their strategies.

Many white people joined the Black Lives Matter protests of 2020 as allies. It seemed as though there was a sudden mass awakening to the fact that racism is real in America. While we certainly need allies in the cause, we need allies who are knowledgeable of the issues, can empathize, and know how to support.

The guidelines for allyship in figure 9.1 are important. Allies can join and actively engage in organizations like SURJ.

4. **Become power brokers.** Committed allies are needed. However, allies are not always in a position of power to change systems. At the interpersonal level, allies can support BIPOC by taking on the struggles as their own, speaking up, and doing their own work. Power brokers, by definition, deliberately affect the distribution of political or economic power by exerting influence. As I mentioned in the introduction, at the height of the Black Lives Matter movement of 2020, we witnessed power brokers quickly making

The Do's and Don'ts of Allyship . . .

- **Do** be open to listening
- **Do** be aware of your implicit biases
- **Do** your research to learn more about the history of the struggle in which you are participating
- **Do** the inner work to figure out a way to acknowledge how you participate in oppressive systems
- **Do** the outer work and figure out how to change the oppressive systems
- **Do** amplify (online and when physically present) the voices of those without your privilege
- **Do** learn how to *listen* and accept criticism with grace, even if it's uncomfortable
- **Do not** expect to be taught or shown. Take it upon yourself to use the tools around you to learn and answer your questions
- **Do not** participate for the gold medal in the "Oppression Olympics" (you don't need to compare how your struggle is just as bad)
- **Do not** behave as though you know best
- **Do not** take credit for the labor of those who are marginalized and did the work before you stepped into the picture
- **Do not** assume that every member of an underinvested group feels oppressed

Figure 9.1. The Do's and Don'ts of Allyship . . .
Source: The Winters Group based on data in "Guide to Allyship" by Amélie Lamont.[12]

decisions to defund police departments, ban chokeholds and the use of tear gas, and update use-of-force rules. A 22-year-old Black woman convinced the *Merriam-Webster* dictionary to change the definition of "racism" to include the structural component. Power brokers hold the key to systemic change.

5. **Stop using "discomfort" as an excuse for not having meaningful conversations about race.** I regularly hear that we do not talk about race because it is uncomfortable. Discomfort is a part of what Robin DiAngelo defines as white fragility. It is uncomfortable because of a lack of knowledge

about racism. It is uncomfortable because the very mention of the word conjures up the good-bad binary. For some, if we do not talk about it, we do not have to address it. For others, the intense emotional response the word elicits renders them speechless. We must talk about racism to dismantle it.

What Should Black People Do?

1. **Use your voice.** It seems that there is now more willingness to listen to the daily inequities that we face in "living while Black." Understand and speak to the structural issues and their domino-effect impact. For example, underfunded schools and schools with staff who perpetuate deficiency stereotypes feeds the prison pipeline, the dismantling of Black family structure, and disproportionate unemployment rates.
2. **Stay vigilant.** Educate yourself on the issues, lobby for change and vote.
3. **Reject the expectation of being a "teacher."** Using your voice does not mean that you should be expected to serve as white people's history books. Unapologetically tell white people to do their own work, if you do not want to serve in that role.
4. **Reframe deficit narratives.** As Black people, we should frame narratives to shift the blame to white supremacy for the inequities and violence against us. For example, rather than explaining that Black people are exhausted, state that racism is exhausting. Or rather than stating that Black people are disproportionately denied loans, note that banks discriminate against Black people in lending. Here are some examples:

Black people are exhausted	→	Racism is exhausting
Black people can't get loans	→	Banks disproportionately deny Black people loans
Black children lag in academic performance	→	Schools are structured to disadvantage Black students
Black people are underrepresented in technology jobs	→	Technology companies fail to attract and retain Black people
Black men are 2.5 times more likely than white men to be killed by police	→	Police are 2.5 times more likely to kill Black men than white men

5. **If you are Black in a position of power and influence, use your power to advance BIPOC.** Too often Black leaders assimilate, fearing losing their own status if they support other Black people.
6. **Take good care.** Engage in self-care, as highlighted in chapter 4. Reject oppressive norms and systems that compromise sense of self. The ideology of white supremacy and systems of racism are real in the workplace and world. Build your capacity to name the systems rather than internalizing them.

What Can Black and White People Do Together?

This is a moment in history where we have the opportunity for real change. It will not be easy and will take commitment and action from enough people who can turn the tide. It must involve learning, unlearning, and relearning because the systems of racism are so very entrenched in the fabric of society. If Black and White people are to work together we will need to:

- **Dialogue.** Learn cross-race dialogue skill as outlined in my books *Inclusive Conversations* and *We Can't Talk About That at Work*. Ensure that our cross-racial conversations are grounded in principles of equity. This means that the voices of the marginalized that have not been heard are amplified and given more priority.
- **Acknowledge that our lived experiences are very different and learn to practice reciprocal empathy.** Empathy is only possible when there is a shared understanding.
- **Create a shared decolonized model of how to dismantle structural racism.** Focus on the systems of oppression rather than programmatic solutions.
- **Collaborate in earnest to understand how elements of racist systems interrelate.** Interrogate together the interlocking elements that contribute to racism. There are too many silos today not working on the bigger systems issues. Grassroots organizations need to be invited into corporate and government spaces to work together on equity-centered solutions.
- **Hold power brokers accountable by identifying specific accountability measures and transparent practices and goals that support racial equity and justice.** Those with power can change policies and practices that disadvantage Black people. They are discoverable, identifiable, and fixable if we have the will to do the work.

CONCLUSION

Reimagining a Just World

I would like to reimagine a new United States of America—an America where Black people are not fatigued because justice is a reality. In some ways it seems simple to dismantle white supremacy; however, I am not so naïve as to believe it is easy. I think we know what to do. I just wonder whether we have the will to do it. In my reimagined world . . .

- The government would officially apologize for slavery and pay reparations.
- White supremacy would be acknowledged and disavowed and there would be concerted and sincere efforts to dismantle it.
- Racism would be understood as a white problem, not a Black one.
- Existing legislation to combat racism would be enforced and not weakened by newer legislation designed to maintain white supremacy.
- Black people's right to vote would not be suppressed by actions such as gerrymandering, closing polling places, and purging voter records.
- Black people would enjoy economic parity.
- Black people could bury the terms "Black tax," "living while Black," and "Black fatigue" because they would no longer be a part of our reality.

- Allies would no longer be needed because equity has been realized.
- We would never see another Black person gunned down by police.
- White people would understand that it is their responsibility to protect Black people from anti-Black racism.
- We would never again see the anguish and pain of Black mothers, fathers, brothers, and sisters who are left to grieve the tragedy of the senseless killing by police of their loved one.
- There would be no more knots of fear in our stomachs every time our Black children or other loved ones left the house because we would not worry that they may not come home alive.
- Police officers would never be acquitted for needlessly killing Black people, and they would serve time commensurate with the crime.
- Black parents' "talk" about law enforcement would be "The police are your friends and they will protect you" rather than "Beware of law enforcement. Do not do anything that would risk your coming home alive."
- Black people could go for a drive without the fear of being stopped for a "missing taillight."
- We would no longer have to ask, "Why are there no Black people in leadership at this organization?"
- Black people would be presumed innocent until proven guilty rather than guilty until proven innocent.
- Black people would not have to navigate life always "on guard," wondering to what extent our race is a factor in any interaction.

- White people would know why Blackface is offensive and would not dismiss such displays as "no big deal."
- White people would invite and expect Black people to "play the race card" when needed.
- Black people could "play the race card" on white people to point out their privilege and fragility.
- White people would not tokenize Black people by expecting us to represent "all" Black people.
- White people would do their own education about racism and not place the emotional toll on Black people to be their teachers.
- Black people would be compensated equitably for their time when White people ask them to be the "Black expert."
- White women would not start crying when the topic of racism is raised, turning the attention to them and away from the Black people who raised the issue.
- We could retire the "Karen" meme because white women would no longer feel entitled to monitor and question the legitimacy of Black people's actions.
- White women would not call Black women "divisive" for wanting to focus on issues unique to Black women.
- Nobody in the organization would say or allow as an excuse, "Our leaders are not ready to talk about race."
- Black people would be able to exercise their First Amendment rights to protest without being teargassed, just like white people who protest with assault weapons and do not have law enforcement engaged.
- "Essential worker" would not mean "sacrificial worker."
- Work environments would really be inclusive and foster a sense of belonging for Black people.

- White people would know better than to "whitesplain" to us about how to respond to racism.
- We would never hear again, "We are looking to hire *qualified* Black people" because the assumption would be that Black people are not inherently less qualified than White people.
- Resilience ("bouncing back") would not be the solution to racism.
- Black people's anger would be accepted as an appropriate response to racism.
- White people would not be bothered by or suspicious of Black people's presence in public spaces. We could have a picnic, rent an Airbnb, or fall asleep in the common area of a college dorm without the police being called.
- To be a tall, dark, Black man would not be threatening to white people.
- Black people could wear our hair any way we choose without risking it being cut off because some white person in power does not like it. We would not need legislation (the CROWN Act) to give us that right.
- White people would not use the excuse of being "uncomfortable" to avoid talking about race. White discomfort would not be prioritized over Black comfort.
- White people's lies would not be more credible than Black people's truths.
- White people would mind their own business when Black people are minding theirs.
- Our children would see themselves portrayed age appropriately in books and other media.
- Teachers would believe that Black children are capable and have unlimited potential.

- Hoodies would be humanized, not criminalized.
- White people would know that being color-blind is not the goal and it is offensive to most Black people. If you are color-blind, you in essence render Black people invisible.
- White people would realize that having Black friends is not an automatic exemption from being a racist.
- White people would universally understand that the Black Lives Matter movement would not be necessary if all lives really mattered.
- Liberty and justice for all would be a reality.

If my reimagined world achieved half of this list, we would be well on our way to eliminating Black fatigue.

I am no longer accepting the things I cannot change. I am changing the things I cannot accept.

—Angela Davis, American political activist, philosopher, academic, Marxist feminist, and author

NOTES

Preface

1. D. Lanham and A. Liu, "Not Just a Typographical Change: Why Brookings Is Capitalizing Black," Brookings, September 23, 2019, https://www.brookings.edu/research/brookingscapitalizesblack/.

2. History.com editors, "Emmett Till," History, December 2, 2009, updated May 2, 2019, https://www.history.com/topics/black-history/emmett-till-1.

3. NewsOne Staff, "83 Black Men and Boys Killed by Police," NewsOne, June 2, 2020, https://newsone.com/playlist/black-men-boy-who-were-killed-by-police/item/1.

Introduction

1. J. Williams, "IM NOT OK : Jumaane Williams on George Floyd, ahmaud arbery and Trump." *YouTube* Video, 4:10. May 28, 2020. https://www.youtube.com/watch?v=YM-lLIt20HM

2. "H.R.5309—116th Congress (2019–2020)," https://www.congress.gov/bill/116th-congress/house-bill/5309/text.

3. R. DiAngelo, *White Fragility* (Boston: Beacon, 2018).

4. J. Baldwin, *The Fire Next Time* (New York: Dial, 1963), 24.

Chapter One

1. "Brown v. Board of Education," Landmark Cases of the U.S. Supreme Court, accessed April 8, 2020, https://www.landmarkcases.org/cases/brown-v-board-of-education.

2. E. N. Winkler, "Children Are Not Colorblind: How Young Children Learn Race," PACE, no. 3 (2009), https://inclusions.org/wp-content/uploads/2017/11/Children-are-Not-Colorblind.pdf.

3. History.com editors, "Niagara Movement," History, December 2, 2009, updated August 21, 2018, https://www.history.com/topics/black-history/niagara-movement.

4. B. Griggs, "A black Yale graduate student took a nap in her dorm's common room. So a white student called police," May 12, 2018, https://www.cnn.com/2018/05/09/us/yale-student-napping-black-trnd/index.html.

5. Open Mic Rochester and City Newspaper, "Frederick Douglass's Rochester," https://rocdouglass.com/.

6. V. M. Massie, "White Women Benefit Most from Affirmative Action and Are among Its Fiercest Opponents," Vox, June 23, 2016, https://www.vox.com/2016/5/25/11682950fisher-supreme-court-white-women-affirmative-action.

7. E. L. Green, M. Apuzzo, and K. Benner, "Trump Officials Reverse Obama's Policy on Affirmative Action in Schools," *New York Times*, July 3, 2018, https://www.nytimes.com/2018/07/03/us/politics/trump-affirmative-action-race-schools.html.

8. A. Brown, "Key Findings on Americans' Views of Race in 2019," Pew Research Center, April 9, 2019, https://www.pewresearch.org/fact-tank/2019/04/09/key-findings-on-americans-views-of-race-in-2019/.

Chapter Two

1. I. X. Kendi, *Stamped from the Beginning: The Definitive History of Racist Ideas in America* (New York: Bold Type Books, 2017).

2. "The 1619 Project," https://www.nytimes.com/interactive/2019/08/14/magazine/1619-america-slavery.html.

3. C. Anderson, *White Rage: The Unspoken Truth of Our Racial Divide* (New York: Bloomsbury, 2017).

4. W. E. B. Du Bois, *Black Reconstruction in America* (New York: Free Press, 1998).

5. M. Rediker, *The Slave Ship: A Human History* (New York: Penguin Books, 2008).

6. H. Zinn, *A People's History of the United States* (New York: Harper Perennial Modern Classics, 2015).

7. N. I. Painter, *The History of White People* (New York: W. W. Norton, 2010).

8. M. F. Winters, *We Can't Talk about That at Work! How to Talk about Race, Religion, Politics, and Other Polarizing Topics* (Oakland, CA: Berrett-Koehler, 2017).

9. M. F. Winters, *Inclusive Conversations: Fostering Equity, Empathy, and Belonging across Differences* (Oakland, CA: Berrett-Koehler, 2020).

10. M. Alexander, *The New Jim Crow: Mass Incarceration in the Age of Colorblindness* (New York: New Press, 2012).

11. J. McWhorter, "'Racist' Is a Tough Little Word," *Atlantic*, July 24, 2019, https://www.theatlantic.com/ideas/archive/2019/07/racism-concept-change/594526/.

12. L. King, "Black History as Anti-racist and Non-racist," in *But I Don't See Color: The Perils, Practices, and Possibilities of Antiracist Education*, ed. Terry Husband (Rotterdam: SensePublishers, 2016), 63–79.

13. O. Jones, "Ibram X Kendi on Why Not Being Racist Is Not Enough," *Guardian*, August 14, 2019, https://www.theguardian.com/world/2019/aug/14/ibram-x-kendi-on-why-not-being-racist-is-not-enough.

14. "Racism Defined," Dismantling Racism Works Web Workbook, January 2020, http://www.dismantlingracism.org/racism-defined.html.

15. "Racism Defined," Dismantling Racism Works Web Workbook, January 2020, http://www.dismantlingracism.org/racism-defined.html.

Chapter Three

1. R. Booth and C. Barr, "Black People Four Times More Likely to Die from Covid-19, ONS Finds," *Guardian*, May 7, 2020, https://www.theguardian.com/world/2020/may/07/black-people-four-times-more-likely-to-die-from-covid-19-ons-finds.

2. M. Kelly, "Civil Rights Legislation and Supreme Court Cases," ThoughtCo., updated November 20, 2019, https://www.thoughtco.com/overview-civil-rights-legislation-supreme-court-104388.

3. J. Ross and National Journal, "African-Americans with College Degrees Are Twice as Likely to Be Unemployed as Other Graduates," *Atlantic*, May 27, 2014, https://www.theatlantic.com/politics/archive/2014/05/african-americans-with-college-degrees-are-twice-as-likely-to-be-unemployed-as-other-graduates/430971/.

4. N. Lakhani, "America Has an Infant Mortality Crisis. Meet the Black Doulas Trying to Change That," *Guardian*, November 25, 2019, https://www.theguardian.com/us-news/2019/nov/25/african-american-doula-collective-mothers-toxic-stress-racism-cleveland-infant-mortality-childbirth.

5. E. Gould, "Stark Black–White Divide in Wages Is Widening Further," *Working Economics Blog*, Economic Policy Institute, February 27, 2019, https://www.epi.org/blog/stark-black-white-divide-in-wages-is-widening-further/.

6. "Median Value of Family Net Worth, by Race or Ethnicity, 2016," Tax Policy Center, March 11, 2019, https://www.taxpolicycenter.org/fiscal-fact/median-value-wealth-race-ff03112019.

7. V. Wilson, "10 Years after the Start of the Great Recession, Black and Asian households Have Yet to Recover Lost Income," *Working Economics Blog*, Economic Policy Institute, September 12, 2018, https://www.epi.org/blog/10-years-after-the-start-of-the-great-recession-black-and-asian-households-have-yet-to-recover-lost-income/.

8. K. Zaw et al., *Women, Race & Wealth*, vol. 1, Research Brief Series (Samuel DuBois Cook Center on Social Equity and Insight Center for Community Economic Development, January 2017), http://www.insightcced.org/wp-content/uploads/2017/01/January2017_ResearchBriefSeries_WomenRaceWealth-Volume1-Pages-1.pdf.

9. C. Collins, D. Asante-Muhammad, J. Hoxie, and S. Terry, "Dreams Deferred," 2019, https://inequality.org/wp-content/uploads/2019/01/IPS_RWD-Report_FINAL-1.15.19.pdf.

10. A. Elejalde-Ruiz, "Hiring Bias Study: Resumes with Black, White, Hispanic Names Treated the Same," *Chicago Tribune*, May 4, 2016, https://www.chicagotribune.com/business/ct-bias-hiring-0504-biz-20160503-story.html.

11. A. Hanks, D. Solomon, and C. E. Weller, "Systematic Inequality," Center for American Progress, February 21, 2018, https://www.americanprogress.org/issues/race/reports/2018/02/21/447051/systematic-inequality/.

12. V. Wilson, "Black Unemployment Is Significantly Higher Than White Unemployment Regardless of Educational Attainment," Economic Policy Institute, December 17, 2015, https://www.epi.org/publication/black-unemployment-educational-attainment/.

13. "Unemployment Rate 3.6 Percent in April 2019, Lowest since December 1969," US Bureau of Labor Statistics, May 8, 2019, https://www.bls.gov/opub/ted/2019/unemployment-rate-3-point-6-percent-in-april-2019-lowest-since-december-1969.htm.

14. A. Glantz and E. Martinez, "Modern-Day Redlining: Banks Discriminate in Lending," Reveal, February 15, 2018, https://www.revealnews.org/article/for-people-of-color-banks-are-shutting-the-door-to-homeownership/.

15. "Demographic Trends and Economic Well-Being," Pew Research Center, June 27, 2016, https://www.pewsocialtrends.org/2016/06/27/1-demographic-trends-and-economic-well-being/.

16. "Community Reinvestment Act," FFIEC, accessed February 27, 2020, https://www.ffiec.gov/cra/.

17. B. Mock, "Is Gentrification a National Emergency?," Bloomberg CityLab, April 5, 2019, https://www.citylab.com/equity/2019/04/where-gentrification-happens-neighborhood-crisis-research/586537/.

18. National Fair Housing Alliance, *The Case for Fair Housing: 2017 Fair Housing Trends Report* (Washington, DC: National Fair Housing Alliance, 2017), 6, https://nationalfairhousing.org/wp-content/uploads/2017/07/TRENDS-REPORT-2017-FINAL.pdf.

19. K. Shakir, "GENTRIFICATION IS "NEGRO REMOVAL": A PARASITICALLY VICIOUS ATTACK AGAINST POC COMMUNITIES," March 6, 2018, https://afropunk.com/2018/03/gentrification-negro-removal-parasitically-vicious-attack-poc-communities/#:~:text=James%20Baldwin%2C%20a%20popular%20figure,of%20social%20media%20and%20YouTube.

20. J. Williams and V. Wilson, "Black Workers Endure Persistent Racial Disparities in Employment Outcomes," Economic Policy Institute, August 27, 2019, https://www.epi.org/publication/labor-day-2019-racial-disparities-in-employment/.

21. Center for Talent Innovation, *Being Black in Corporate America: An Intersectional Exploration* (Center for Talent Innovation, 2019), https://www.talentinnovation.org/_private/assets/BeingBlack-KeyFindings-CTI.pdf.

22. "Who We Are," Ascend, accessed February 21, 2020, https://www.ascendleadership.org/page/whoweare.

23. M. Gee, "Why Aren't Black Employees Getting More White-Collar Jobs?," *Harvard Business Review*, February 28, 2018, https://hbr.org/2018/02/why-arent-black-employees-getting-more-white-collar-jobs.

24. A. Brown and S. Atske, "Blacks Have Made Gains in U.S. Political Leadership, but Gaps Remain," Pew Research Center, January 18, 2019, https://www.pewresearch.org/fact-tank/2019/01/18/blacks-have-made-gains-in-u-s-political-leadership-but-gaps-remain/.

25. "Hispanic-American Representatives, Senators, Delegates, and Resident Commissioners by Congress, 1822–Present," History, Art & Archives, US House of Representatives, accessed February 5, 2020, https://history.house.gov/Exhibitions-and-Publications/HAIC/Historical-Data/Hispanic-American-Representatives,-Senators,-Delegates,-and-Resident-Commissioners-by-Congress/.

26. "Historical Data," History, Art & Archives, US House of Representatives, accessed February 5, 2020, https://history.house.gov/Exhibitions-and-Publications/APA/Historical-Data/Historical-Data/.

27. D. Solomon, C. Maxwell, and A. Castro, "Systematic Inequality and Economic Opportunity," August 7, 2019, https://www.americanprogress.org/issues/race/reports/2019/08/07/472910/systematic-inequality-economic-opportunity/.

28. History.com editors, "Voting Rights Act of 1965," History, November 9, 2009, updated June 6, 2019, https://www.history.com/topics/black-history/voting-rights-act.

29. "Top Court Strikes Down Part of Voting Rights Act," CNBC, June 25, 2013, https://www.cnbc.com/id/100842178.

30. R. Ray and M. Whitlock, "Setting the record straight on Black voter turnout," September 12, 2019, https://www.brookings.edu/blog/how-we-rise/2019/09/12/setting-the-record-straight-on-black-voter-turnout/.

31. D. Solomon, C. Maxwell, and A. Castro, "Systematic Inequality and Economic Opportunity," August 7, 2019, https://www.americanprogress.org/issues/race/reports/2019/08/07/472910/systematic-inequality-economic-opportunity/.

32. D. Solomon, C. Maxwell, and A. Castro, "Systematic Inequality and Economic Opportunity," August 7, 2019, https://www.americanprogress.org/issues/race/reports/2019/08/07/472910/systematic-inequality-economic-opportunity/.

33. D. Solomon, C. Maxwell, and A. Castro, "Systematic Inequality and Economic Opportunity," August 7, 2019, https://www.americanprogress.org/issues/race/reports/2019/08/07/472910/systematic-inequality-economic-opportunity/.

34. J. Cobb, "The Supreme Court Just Legitimized a Cornerstone Element of Voter Suppression," *New Yorker*, July 3, 2019, https://www.newyorker.com/news/daily-comment/the-supreme-court-just-legitimized-a-cornerstone-element-of-voter-suppression).

35. L. Noe-Bustamante, A. Budiman, and M. H. Lopez, "Where Latinos Have the Most Eligible Voters in the 2020 Election," Pew Research Center, January 31, 2020, https://www.pewresearch.org/fact-tank/2020/01/31/where-latinos-have-the-most-eligible-voters-in-the-2020-election/.

36. J. Boschma and R. Brownstein, "Students of Color Are Much More Likely to Attend Schools Where Most of Their Peers Are Poor," *Atlantic*, February 29, 2016, https://www.theatlantic.com/education/archive/2016/02/concentration-poverty-american-schools/471414/.

37. E. Lieb, "Which Came First: Segregated Schools or Segregated Neighborhoods?," Bloomberg CityLab, February 2, 2017, https://www.citylab.com/equity/2017/02/how-segregated-schools-built-segregated-cities/515373/.

38. N. McArdle and D. Acevedo-Garcia, "Consequences of Segregation for Children's Opportunity and Wellbeing" (paper presented at "A Shared Future: Fostering Communities of Inclusion in an Era of Inequality," Harvard Joint Center for Housing Studies, April 2017), https://www.jchs.harvard.edu/sites/default/files/a_shared_future_consequences_of_segregation_for_children.pdf.

39. A. S. Wells, L. Fox, and D. Cordova-Cobo, "How Racially Diverse Schools and Classrooms Can Benefit All Students," Century Foundation, February 9, 2016, https://tcf.org/content/report/how-racially-diverse-schools-and-classrooms-can-benefit-all-students/?agreed=1&session=1.

40. "Nonwhite School Districts Get $23 Billion Less Than White Districts Despite Serving the Same Number of Students," EdBuild, accessed February 27, 2020, https://edbuild.org/content/23-billion.

41. L. Dingerson, *Confronting the Education Debt: We Owe Billions to Black, Brown and Low-Income Students and Their Schools* (Alliance to Reclaim Our Schools, September 2018), http://educationdebt.reclaimourschools.org/wp-content/uploads/2018/08/Confronting-the-Education-Debt_FullReport.pdf.

42. C. Jencks and M. Phillips, "The Black-White Test Score Gap: Why It Persists and What Can Be Done," Brookings, March 1, 1998, https://www.brookings.edu/articles/the-black-white-test-score-gap-why-it-persists-and-what-can-be-done/.

43. "K-12 Disparity Facts and Statistics," https://uncf.org/pages/k-12-disparity-facts-and-stats.

44. "K-12 Disparity Facts and Statistics," https://uncf.org/pages/k-12-disparity-facts-and-stats.

45. "K-12 Disparity Facts and Statistics," https://uncf.org/pages/k-12-disparity-facts-and-stats.

46. R. Miller, "Betsy DeVos Uses a Racist Research Study to Defend Rescinding Obama-Era Discipline Guidance," Progressive, April 11, 2019, https://progressive.org/public-school-shakedown/betsy-devos-uses-racist-research-study-miller-190411/.

47. N. Morrison, "Black Students 'Face Racial Bias' in School Discipline," *Forbes*, April 5, 2019, https://www.forbes.com/sites/nickmorrison/2019/04/05/black-students-face-racial-bias-in-school-discipline/#3022e77136d5.

48. "History of Lynchings," NAACP, accessed February 27, 2020, https://www.naacp.org/history-of-lynchings/.

49. F. Edwards, H. Lee, and M. Esposito, "Risk of Being Killed by Police Use of Force in the United States by Age, Race–Ethnicity, and Sex," *National Academy of Sciences* 116, no. 34 (2019): 1679–16798, https://doi.org/10.1073/pnas.1821204116.

50. B. Mock, "Reversing the 'Reverse Racism' Effect," Bloomberg CityLab, February 8, 2017, https://www.citylab.com/equity/2017/02/is-reverse-racism-among-police-real/513503/.

51. NewsOne Staff, "83 Black Men and Boys Killed by Police," NewsOne, June 2, 2020, https://newsone.com/playlist/black-men-boy-who-were-killed-by-police/item/1/.

52. A. Sastry and K. G. Bates, "When LA Erupted in Anger: A Look Back at the Rodney King Riots," NPR, April 26, 2017, https://www.npr.org/2017/04/26/524744989/when-la-erupted-in-anger-a-look-back-at-the-rodney-king-riots.

53. J. Fritsch, "The Diallo Verdict: The Overview; 4 Officers in Diallo Shooting Are Acquitted of All Charges," *New York Times*, February 26, 2000, https://www.nytimes.com/2000/02/26/nyregion/diallo-verdict-overview-4-officers-diallo-shooting-are-acquitted-all-charges.html.

54. "Booker, Harris, Scott Lead Unanimous Passage of Federal Anti-lynching Legislation," Cory Booker's Senate website, February 14, 2019, https://www.booker.senate.gov/news/press/booker-harris-scott-lead-unanimous-passage-of-federal-anti-lynching-legislation.

55. B. Everett, "Rand Paul Battles Kamala Harris and Cory Booker on Anti-lynching Bill," Politico, June 4, 2020, https://www.politico.com/news/2020/06/04/rand-paul-anti-lynching-bill-301617.

56. L. A. Greenfield and S. K. Smith, *American Indians and Crime* (Washington, DC: Bureau of Justice Statistics, February 1999), https://bjs.gov/content/pub/pdf/aic.pdf.

57. J. Gramlich, "The Gap between the Number of Blacks and Whites in Prison Is Shrinking," Pew Research Center, April 30, 2019, https://www.pewresearch.org/fact-tank/2019/04/30/shrinking-gap-between-number-of-blacks-and-whites-in-prison/.

58. S. R. Gross, M. Possley, and K. Stephens, *Race and Wrongful Convictions in the United States* (Irvine, CA: National Registry of Exonerations, March 7, 2017), http://www.law.umich.edu/special/exoneration/Documents/Race_and_Wrongful_Convictions.pdf.

59. E. Sun, "The Dangerous Racialization of Crime in U.S. News Media," Center for American Progress, August 29, 2018, https://www.americanprogress.org/issues/criminal-justice/news/2018/08/29/455313/dangerous-racialization-crime-u-s-news-media/.

60. L. Collier, "Incarceration Nation," *Monitor on Psychology* 45, no. 9 (2014), http://www.apa.org/monitor/2014/10/incarceration.

61. M. Alexander, *The New Jim Crow: Mass Incarceration in the Age of Colorblindness* (New York: New Press, 2012).

Chapter Four

1. "Fannie Lou Hamer Quotes," BrainyQuote, accessed March 9, 2020, https://www.brainyquote.com/quotes/fannie_lou_hamer_143110.

2. "About," Nap Ministry, accessed June 20, 2020, https://thenapministry.wordpress.com/about/.

3. D. Vergano and K. Goba, "Why the Coronavirus Is Killing Black Americans at Outsize Rates across the US," BuzzFeed, April 10, 2020, https://www.buzzfeednews.com/article/danvergano/coronavirus-black-americans-covid19.

4. "African American Health Disparities Compared to Non-Hispanic Whites," Families USA, January 17, 2019, https://familiesusa.org/resources/african-american-health-disparities-compared-to-non-hispanic-whites/.

5. "Breast Cancer Rates among Black Women and White Women," Centers for Disease Control and Prevention, September 13, 2018, https://www.cdc.gov/cancer/dcpc/research/articles/breast_cancer_rates_women.htm.

6. M. Hostetter and S. Klein, "In Focus: Reducing Racial Disparities in Health Care by Confronting Racism," Commonwealth Fund, September 27, 2018, https://www.commonwealthfund.org/publications/newsletter-article/2018/sep/focus-reducing-racial-disparities-health-care-confronting.

7. E. Arias and J. Xu, "United States Life Tables, 2017," National Vital Statistics Reports 68, no. 7 (2019), https://www.cdc.gov/nchs/data/nvsr/nvsr68/nvsr68_07-508.pdf.

8. R. Carlson, "The Racial Life Expectancy Gap in the U.S.," Balance, updated March 8, 2019, https://www.thebalance.com/the-racial-life-expectancy-gap-in-the-u-s-4588898.

9. E. Arias and J. Xu, "United States Life Tables, 2017," *National Vital Statistics Reports* 68, no. 7 (2019), https://www.cdc.gov/nchs/data/nvsr/nvsr68/nvsr68_07-508.pdf.

10. R. Lavizzo-Mourey and D. Williams, "Being Black Is Bad for Your Health," *U.S. News*, April 14, 2016, https://www.usnews.com/opinion/blogs/policy-dose/articles/2016-04-14/theres-a-huge-health-equity-gap-between-whites-and-minorities.

11. E. Arias and J. Xu, "United States Life Tables, 2017," National Vital Statistics Reports 68, no. 7 (2019), https://www.cdc.gov/nchs/data/nvsr/nvsr68/nvsr68_07-508.pdf.

12. V. M. Mays, S. D. Cochran, and N. W. Barnes, "Race, Race-Based Discrimination, and Health Outcomes among African Americans," *Annual Review of Psychology* 58 (2007): 201–225, https://doi.org/10.1146/annurev.psych.57.102904.190212.

13. E. Dermendzhiyska, "Rejection Kills," Aeon, April 30, 2019, https://aeon.co/essays/health-warning-social-rejection-doesnt-only-hurt-it-kills.

14. "Social Determinants of Health," Office of Disease Prevention and Health Promotion, accessed March 9, 2020, https://www.healthypeople.gov/2020/topics-objectives/topic/social-determinants-of-health.

15. L. Knox, "New Study Shows Racism May Shorten Black Americans' Lifespans," NBC News, February 5, 2020, https://www.nbcnews.com/news/nbcblk/new-study-shows-racism-may-shorten-black-americans-lifespans-n1128351.

16. L. Knox, "New Study Shows Racism May Shorten Black Americans' Lifespans," NBC News, February 5, 2020, https://www.nbcnews.com/news/nbcblk/new-study-shows-racism-may-shorten-black-americans-lifespans-n1128351.

17. C. G. Colen et al., "Racial Disparities in Health among Nonpoor African Americans and Hispanics: The Role of Acute and Chronic Discrimination," *Social Science and Medicine* 199 (2018): 167–180, https://doi.org/10.1016/j.socscimed.2017.04.051.

18. M. Park, "Police Shootings: Trials, Convictions Are Rare for Officers," CNN, October 3, 2018, https://www.cnn.com/2017/05/18/us/police-involved-shooting-cases/index.html.

19. D. Criss and A. Vera, "Three Black People Checked Out of Their Airbnb Rental. Then Someone Called the Police on Them," CNN, May 10, 2018, https://www.cnn.com/2018/05/07/us/airbnb-police-called-trnd/index.html.

20. T. B. Brown, "Why Didn't the Store Just Let Oprah Buy the $38,000 Handbag?," NPR, August 10, 2013, https://www.npr.org/sections/codeswitch/2013/08/10/210574193/why-didnt-the-store-just-let-oprah-buy-the-38-000-handbag.

21. M. Zaveri, "Black Man Killed by Officer in Alabama Mall Shooting Was Not the Gunman, Police Now Say," *New York Times*, November 24, 2018, https://www.nytimes.com/2018/11/24/us/alabama-mall-shooting.html.

22. Black Athlete Says He Was Wrongly Detained, Threatened by Illinois Police Officers at Rest Stop While Traveling with College Swim Team," *Chicago Tribune*, February 17, 2020, https://www.chicagotribune.com/news/breaking/ct-jaylan-butler-illinois-police-false-arrest-lawsuit-20200216-ovwhbbg7cbfinjw5txl7enugze-story.html.

23. R. T. Carter, "Racism and Psychological and Emotional Injury: Recognizing and Assessing Race-Based Traumatic Stress," *Counseling Psychologist* 35, no. 1 (January 2007): 13–105, https://doi.org/10.1177/0011000006292033.

24. J. A. DeGruy, *Post Traumatic Slave Syndrome: America's Legacy of Enduring Injury and Healing* (n.p.: Joy DeGruy Publications, 2005), 105.

25. "Historical Trauma and Cultural Healing," University of Minnesota Extension, accessed October 10, 2019, https://extension.umn.edu/mental-health/historical-trauma-and-cultural-healing#what-is-historical-trauma?-378610.

26. J. Silverstein, "How Racism Is Bad for Our Bodies," *Atlantic*, March 12, 2013, https://www.theatlantic.com/health/archive/2013/03/how-racism-is-bad-for-our-bodies/273911/.

27. "Inheriting Racist Disparities in Health: Epigenetics and the Transgenerational Effects of White Racism," *Critical Philosophy of Race* 1, no. 2 (2013): 190–218, https://doi.org/10.5325/critphilrace.1.2.0190.

28. K. M. Bridges, "Implicit Bias and Racial Disparities in Health Care," American Bar Association, accessed March 16, 2020, https://www.americanbar.org/groups/crsj/publications/human_rights_magazine_home/the-state-of-healthcare-in-the-united-states/racial-disparities-in-health-care/.

29. K. N. Ray et al., "Disparities in Time Spent Seeking Medical Care in the United States," *JAMA Internal Medicine* 175, no. 12 (2015): 1983–1986, https://doi.org/10.1001/jamainternmed.2015.4468.

30. L. Rapaport, "Nonwhite Patients Get Less Pain Relief in U.S. Emergency Rooms," *Physician's Weekly*, July 2, 2019, https://www.physiciansweekly.com/nonwhite-patients-get-less/.

31. K. M. Bridges, "Implicit Bias and Racial Disparities in Health Care," American Bar Association, accessed March 16, 2020, https://www.americanbar.org/groups/crsj/publications/human_rights_magazine_home/the-state-of-healthcare-in-the-united-states/racial-disparities-in-health-care/.

32. K. M. Bridges, "Implicit Bias and Racial Disparities in Health Care," American Bar Association, accessed March 16, 2020, https://www.americanbar.org/groups/crsj/publications/human_rights_magazine_home/the-state-of-healthcare-in-the-united-states/racial-disparities-in-health-care/.

33. J. C. Williams, "Black Americans Don't Trust Our Healthcare System—Here's Why," The Hill, August 24, 2017, https://thehill.com/blogs/pundits-blog/healthcare/347780-black-americans-dont-have-trust-in-our-healthcare-system.

34. N. Martin and R. Montagne, "Black Mothers Keep Dying after Giving Birth. Shalon Irving's Story Explains Why," NPR, December 7, 2017, https://www.npr.org/2017/12/07/568948782/black-mothers-keep-dying-after-giving-birth-shalon-irvings-story-explains-why.

35. "About the IAT," Project Implicit, accessed March 16, 2020, https://implicit.harvard.edu/implicit/iatdetails.html.

36. K. Brooks, "Research Shows Food Deserts More Abundant in Minority Neighborhoods," *Johns Hopkins Magazine*, Spring 2014, https://hub.jhu.edu/magazine/2014/spring/racial-food-deserts/.

37. V. R. Newkirk II, "Trump's EPA Concludes Environmental Racism Is Real," *Atlantic*, February 28, 2019, https://www.theatlantic.com/politics/archive/2018/02/the-trump-administration-finds-that-environmental-racism-is-real/554315/.

38. S. L. Hayes et al., "Reducing Racial and Ethnic Disparities in Access to Care: Has the Affordable Care Act Made a Difference?," Commonwealth Fund, August 24, 2017, https://www.commonwealthfund.org/publications/issue-briefs/2017/aug/reducing-racial-and-ethnic-disparities-access-care-has.

39. S. Artiga, K. Orgera, and A. Damico, "Changes in Health Coverage by Race and Ethnicity since the ACA, 2010–2018," Kaiser Family Foundation, March 5, 2020, https://www.kff.org/disparities-policy/issue-brief/changes-in-health-coverage-by-race-and-ethnicity-since-the-aca-2010-2018/.

40. "Black/African American," National Alliance on Mental Illness, accessed October 18, 2019, https://www.nami.org/find-support/diverse-communities/african-americans.

41. "Health Disparities: African-American or Black Population," Cigna, 2016, https://www.cigna.com/static/www-cigna-com/docs/health-care-providers/african-american-health-disparities.pdf.

42. K. Armstrong et al., "Racial/Ethnic Differences in Physician Distrust in the United States" *American Journal of Public Health* 97, no. 7 (2007): 1283–1289, https://doi.org/10.2105/AJPH.2005.080762.

43. "Coronavirus: France Racism Row over Doctors' Africa Testing Comments," BBC, April 3, 2020, https://www.bbc.com/news/world-europe-52151722.

44. R. Skloot, *The Immortal Life of Henrietta Lacks* (New York: Crown, 2010).

45. M. Mills, review of *Medical Apartheid: The Dark History of Medical Experimentation on Black Americans from Colonial Times to the Present*, by Harriet A. Washington, *Journal of African American History* 94, no. 1 (2009): 101–103, https://www.jstor.org/stable/25610054.

46. V. B. Jernigan et al., "An Examination of Cultural Competence Training in US Medical Education Guided by the Tool for Assessing Cultural Competence Training," *Journal of Health Disparities Research and Practice* 9, no. 3 (2016): 150–167.

47. M. Trent, "AAP Issues First Policy on Racism's Impact on Child Health and How to Address It," AAP News, July 29, 2019, https://www.aappublications.org/news/2019/07/29/racism072919.

48. "Importance of Religion in One's Life by Race/Ethnicity," Pew Research Center, accessed April 27, 2020, https://www.pewforum.org/religious-landscape-study/compare/importance-of-religion-in-ones-life/by/racial-and-ethnic-composition/.

49. J. Diamant, "Blacks More Likely Than Others in U.S. to Read the Bible Regularly, See It as God's Word," Pew Research Center, May 7, 2018, https://www.pewresearch.org/fact-tank/2018/05/07/blacks-more-likely-than-others-in-u-s-to-read-the-bible-regularly-see-it-as-gods-word/.

50. R. V. Magee, *The Inner Work of Racial Justice: Healing Ourselves and Transforming Our Communities through Mindfulness* (New York: TarcherPerigee, 2019), 6.

51. "Historical Perspective," Safe Black Space, accessed April 4, 2020, https://www.safeblackspace.org/about-us, accessed April 4, 2020.

52. T. Subramanian, "Managing the Toll of DEI Work: Reclaiming 'Resilience' & Moving from Paradox to Progress," Inclusion Solution, January 23, 2020, emphasis in original, http://www.theinclusionsolution.me/managing-the-toll-of-dei-work-reclaiming-resilience-moving-from-paradox-to-progress/.

Chapter Five

1. "Attitudes on Same-Sex Marriage," Pew Research Center, May 14, 2019, https://www.pewforum.org/fact-sheet/changing-attitudes-on-gay-marriage/.

2. D. Cox, R. Lienesch, and R. P. Jones, "Who Sees Discrimination? Attitudes on Sexual Orientation, Gender Identity, Race, and Immigration Status," Public Religion Research Institute, June 21, 2017, https://www.prri.org/research/americans-views-discrimination-immigrants-blacks-lgbt-sex-marriage-immigration-reform/.

3. C. Poitras, "The 'Global Closet' Is Huge—Vast Majority of World's Lesbian, Gay, Bisexual Population Hide Orientation, YSPH Study Finds," Yale School of Medicine, June 13, 2019, https://medicine.yale.edu/news-article/20510/.

4. E. Kozuch, "HRC Report: Startling Data Reveals Half of LGBTQ Employees in the U.S. Remain Closeted at Work," Human Rights Campaign, June 25, 2018, https://www.hrc.org/blog/hrc-report-startling-data-reveals-half-of-lgbtq-employees-in-us-remain-clos.

5. P. Williams, "In Landmark Case, Supreme Court Rules LGBTQ Workers Are Protected from Job discrimination," NBC News, June 15, 2020, https://www.nbcnews.com/politics/supreme-court/supreme-court-rules-existing-civil-rights-law-protects-gay-lesbian-n1231018.

6. J. H. Katz, "Heterosexual Privilege: Owning My Advantage, Uncovering My Collusion," *Cultural Diversity at Work* 10, no. 2 (November 1997): 7.

7. K. Crenshaw, "Demarginalizing the Intersection of Race and Sex: A Black Feminist Critique of Antidiscrimination Doctrine, Feminist Theory and Antiracist Politics," *University of Chicago Legal Forum*, no. 1 (1989): 139–167, https://chicagounbound.uchicago.edu/uclf/vol1989/iss1/8.

8. S. Allen, "1 in 5 Non-binary People Denied Medical Treatment Based on Their Identity," Daily Beast, January 10, 2019, https://www.thedailybeast.com/1-in-5-non-binary-people-denied-medical-treatment-based-on-their-identity.

9. S. McBride, "HRC Releases Annual Report on Epidemic of Anti-transgender Violence," Human Rights Campaign, November 18, 2019, https://www.hrc.org/blog/hrc-releases-annual-report-on-epidemic-of-anti-transgender-violence-2019.

10. C. L. Gonzalez, "Study: Women of Color Living in Poverty Face Highest Risk of Eviction," Colorlines, April 9, 2018, https://www.colorlines.com/articles/study-women-color-living-poverty-face-highest-risk-eviction.

11. M. Desmond, "Poor Black Women Are Evicted at Alarming Rates, Setting Off a Chain of Hardship," policy research brief, MacArthur Foundation, March 2014, https://www.macfound.org/media/files/HHM_Research_Brief_-_Poor_Black_Women_Are_Evicted_at_Alarming_Rates.pdf.

12. "Why Eviction Matters," Eviction Lab, accessed April 20, 2020, https://evictionlab.org/why-eviction-matters/.

13. C. L. Gonzalez, "Study: Women of Color Living in Poverty Face Highest Risk of Eviction," Colorlines, April 9, 2018, https://www.colorlines.com/articles/study-women-color-living-poverty-face-highest-risk-eviction.

14. H. Matthews et al., *Implementing the Child Care and Development Block Grant Reauthorization: A Guide for States* (Washington, DC: National Women's Law Center and Center for Law and Social Policy, 2017), 2, https://files.eric.ed.gov/fulltext/ED561773.pdf.

15. K. Capps, "A Brief History of Donald Trump's War on Welfare," Bloomberg CityLab, April 12, 2018, https://www.citylab.com/equity/2018/04/trump-work-requirements-housing-medicaid-snap-federal-aid/557747/.

16. C. R. Emery, "I Am a Black Woman with a Disability. Hear Me Roar," *Time*, July 20, 2016, https://time.com/4401986/black-disabled-woman-power/.

Chapter Six

1. C. Maxwell and D. Solomon, "Mass Incarceration, Stress, and Black Infant Mortality," Center for American Progress, June 5, 2018, https://www.americanprogress.org/issues/race/reports/2018/06/05/451647/mass-incarceration-stress-black-infant-mortality/.

2. K. Patrick, "National Snapshot: Poverty Among Women & Families, 2016," fact sheet, National Women's Law Center, September 2017, https://nwlc.org/wp-content/uploads/2017/09/Poverty-Snapshot-Factsheet-2017.pdf.

3. M. S. Jacobs, "The Violent State: Black Women's Invisible Struggle against Police Violence," *William and Mary Journal of Race, Gender, and Social Justice* 24, no. 1 (2017): 39–100, https://scholarship.law.wm.edu/wmjowl/vol24/iss1/4.

4. K. Crenshaw, "Demarginalizing the Intersection of Race and Sex: A Black Feminist Critique of Antidiscrimination Doctrine, Feminist Theory and Antiracist Politics," *University of Chicago Legal Forum*, no. 1 (1989): 139–167, https://chicagounbound.uchicago.edu/uclf/vol1989/iss1/8.

5. African American Policy Forum and Center for Intersectionality and Social Policy Studies, *Say Her Name: Resisting Police Brutality against Black Women* (New York: African American Policy Forum and Center for Intersectionality and Social Policy Studies, July 2015), http://static1.squarespace.com/static/53f20d90e4b0b80451158d8c/t/560c068ee4b0af26f72741df/1443628686535/AAPF_SMN_Brief_Full_singles-min.pdf.

6. "Black Women & Domestic Violence," Blackburn Center, February 26, 2020, https://www.blackburncenter.org/post/2020/02/26/black-women-domestic-violence.

7. K. W. Savali, "Black Women Have Fought Tirelessly to Protect Our Communities While Placing Our Lives on the Back Burner. No More. It's Time to Prioritize Ourselves," *Essence*, November 8, 2018, https://www.essence.com/news/politics/a-culture-of-silence/.

8. J. A. Degruy, *Post Traumatic Slave Syndrome: America's Legacy of Enduring Injury and Healing* (n.p.: Joy Degruy Publications, 2005), 9.

9. K. Cox and J. Diamant, "Black Men Are Less Religious Than Black Women, but More Religious Than White Women and Men," Pew Research Center, September 26, 2018, https://www.pewresearch.org/fact-tank/2018/09/26/black-men-are-less-religious-than-black-women-but-more-religious-than-white-women-and-men/.

10. C. G. Ellison, M. A. Musick, and A. K. Henderson, "Balm in Gilead: Racism, Religious Involvement, and Psychological Distress among African-American Adults," *Journal for the Scientific Study of Religion* 47, no. 2 (2008): 291–309, https://www.jstor.org/stable/20486913.

11. B. Kesslen, "Aunt Jemima Brand to Change Name, Remove Image That Quaker Says Is 'Based on a Racial Stereotype,'" NBC News, June 17, 2020, https://www.nbcnews.com/news/us-news/aunt-jemima-brand-will-change-name-remove-image-quaker-says-n1231260.

12. A. G. Bauer et al., "Do Black Women's Religious Beliefs about Body Image Influence Their Confidence in Their Ability to Lose Weight?," *Preventing Chronic Disease* 14 (2017), http://dx.doi.org/10.5888/pcd14.170153.

13. G. H. Awad et al., "Beauty and Body Image Concerns among African American College Women," *Journal of Black Psychology* 41, no. 6 (2015): 540–564, https://doi.org/10.1177/0095798414550864.

14. S. Reidy and M. Kanigiri, "How Are Ethnic Hairstyles Really Viewed in the Workplace?," ILR School, Cornell University, 2016, https://digitalcommons.ilr.cornell.edu/cgi/viewcontent.cgi?article=1133&context=student.

15. A. Folley, "Gabrielle Union Reportedly Fired from 'America's Got Talent' after Being Told Her Hairstyles Were 'Too Black': Report," The Hill, November 27, 2019, https://thehill.com/blogs/in-the-know/in-the-know/472362-gabrielle-union-told-her-hairstyles-were-too-black-for-americas.

16. "Black Women and the Wage Gap," fact sheet, National Partnership for Women and Families, March 2020, https://www.nationalpartnership.org/our-work/resources/economic-justice/fair-pay/african-american-women-wage-gap.pdf.

17. S. O'Brien, "Here's How the Wage Gap Affects Black Women," CNBC, August 22, 2019, https://www.cnbc.com/2019/08/22/heres-how-the-gender-wage-gap-affects-this-minority-group.html.

18. A. Hegewisch and H. Hartmann, "The Gender Wage Gap: 2018 Earnings Differences by Race and Ethnicity," Institute for Women's Policy Research, March 7, 2019, https://iwpr.org/publications/gender-wage-gap-2018/.

19. N. Banks, "Black Women's Labor Market History Reveals Deep-Seated Race and Gender Discrimination," *Working Economics Blog*, Economic Policy Institute, February 19, 2019, https://www.epi.org/blog/black-womens-labor-market-history-reveals-deep-seated-race-and-gender-discrimination/.

20. G. B. White, "Black Women: Supporting Their Families—with Few Resources," *Atlantic*, June 12, 2017, https://www.theatlantic.com/business/archive/2017/06/black-women-economy/530022/.

21. N. Banks, "Black Women's Labor Market History Reveals Deep-Seated Race and Gender Discrimination," *Working Economics Blog*, Economic Policy Institute, February 19, 2019, https://www.epi.org/blog/black-womens-labor-market-history-reveals-deep-seated-race-and-gender-discrimination/.

22. Center for Talent Innovation, *Being Black in Corporate America: An Intersectional Exploration* (Center for Talent Innovation, 2019), https://fearlesstalentdev.com/wp-content/uploads/2019/12/Being-Black-KeyFindings-Center-Talent-Innovation.pdf.

23. B. J. Harris, "Demystifying Internalized Oppression: On Being an 'Angry Black Woman,'" Inclusion Solution, August 15, 2019, http://www.theinclusionsolution.me/demystifying-internalized-oppression-on-being-an-angry-black-woman/.

24. D. J. Travis and J. Thorpe-Moscon, *Day-to-Day Experiences of Emotional Tax among Women and Men of Color in the Workplace* (Catalyst, February 15, 2018), https://www.catalyst.org/wp-content/uploads/2019/02/emotionaltax.pdf.

25. D. J. Travis, J. Thorpe-Moscon, and C. McCluney, "Emotional Tax: How Black Women and Men Pay More at Work and How Leaders Can Take Action," Catalyst, October 11, 2016, https://www.catalyst.org/research/emotional-tax-how-black-women-and-men-pay-more-at-work-and-how-leaders-can-take-action/.

26. "Racial and Gender Bias at Work Harmful for Women of Color and their Health," February 15, 2018, https://www.catalyst.org/media-release/racial-and-gender-bias-at-work-harmful-for-women-of-color-and-their-health/.

27. D. J. Travis and J. Thorpe-Moscon, Day-to-Day Experiences of Emotional Tax among Women and Men of Color in the Workplace (Catalyst, February 15, 2018) 15. https://www.catalyst.org/wp-content/uploads/2019/02/emotionaltax.pdf.

28. McKinsey & Company and Lean In, *Women in the Workplace, 2019*, (McKinsey & Company and Lean In, 2019), https://wiw-report.s3.amazonaws.com/Women_in_the_Workplace_2019_print.pdf.

29. M. Cheng, "Why Minority Women Now Control Nearly Half of All Women-Run Businesses," *Inc.*, November 2018, https://www.inc.com/magazine/201811/michelle-cheng/minority-women-entrepreneur-founder-womenable.html.

30. D. W. Sue, *Microaggressions in Everyday Life: Race, Gender, and Sexual Orientation* (Hoboken, NJ: Wiley).

31. E. L. J. Bell Smith and S. M. Nkomo, *Our Separate Ways: Black and White Women and the Struggle for Professional Identity* (Boston: Harvard Business Review Press, 2001).

32. "An Examination of the 2016 Electorate, Based on Validated Voters," Pew Research Center, August 9, 2018, https://www.people-press.org/2018/08/09/an-examination-of-the-2016-electorate-based-on-validated-voters/.

33. R. E. Cargle, "When Feminism Is White Supremacy in Heels," *Harper's Bazaar*, August 16, 2018, https://www.harpersbazaar.com/culture/politics/a22717725/what-is-toxic-white-feminism/.

34. R. DiAngelo, *White Fragility* (Boston: Beacon, 2018).

35. J. Wiggins and K. J. Anderson, *From Sabotage to Support: A New Vision for Feminist Solidarity in the Workplace* (Oakland, CA: Berrett-Koehler, 2019), 90.

36. D. R. Hekman et al., "Does Diversity-Valuing Behavior Result in Diminished Performance Ratings for Non-white and Female Leaders?," Academy of Management Journal 60, no. 2 (2016): 771–797, https://doi.org/10.5465/amj.2014.0538.

37. S. K. Johnson and D. R. Hekman, "Women and Minorities Are Penalized for Promoting Diversity," *Harvard Business Review*, March 23, 2016, https://hbr.org/2016/03/women-and-minorities-are-penalized-for-promoting-diversity.

38. J. A. Degruy, *Post Traumatic Slave Syndrome: America's Legacy of Enduring Injury and Healing* (n.p.: Joy Degruy Publications, 2005).

39. J. Wilson, "The Meaning of #BlackGirlMagic, and How You Can Get Some of It," HuffPost, January 12, 2016, https://www.huffpost.com/entry/what-is-black-girl-magic-video_n_5694dad4e4b086bc1cd517f4.

40. F. Jones, "For CaShawn Thompson, Black Girl Magic Was Always the Truth," Beacon Broadside, February 8, 2019, https://www.beaconbroadside.com/broadside/2019/02/for-cashawn-thompson-black-girl-magic-was-always-the-truth.html.

Chapter Seven

1. R. Ellison, *Invisible Man* (New York: Vintage International, 1995).

2. R. Ellison, *Invisible Man* (New York: Vintage International, 1995), 3.

3. D. W. Griffith, dir., *The Birth of a Nation* (Epoch Producing, 1915).

4. J. R. Winters, *Hope Draped in Black: Race, Melancholy, and the Agony of Progress* (Durham, NC: Duke University Press, 2016).

5. J. R. Winters, Hope Draped in Black: Race, Melancholy, and the Agony of Progress (Durham, NC: Duke University Press, 2016), 138.

6. D. J. Travis and J. Thorpe-Moscon, *Day-to-Day Experiences of Emotional Tax among Women and Men of Color in the Workplace* (Catalyst, February 15, 2018), https://www.catalyst.org/wp-content/uploads/2019/02/emotionaltax.pdf.

7. M. Dittmann, "Standing Tall Pays Off, Study Finds," *Monitor on Psychology* 35, no. 7 (2004), http://www.apa.org/monitor/julaug04/standing.

8. T. Jacobs, "The Problem with Being Tall, Male, and Black," *Pacific Standard*, February 26, 2018, https://psmag.com/social-justice/the-problem-with-being-tall-male-and-black.

9. "Humanize My Hoodie," Born Leaders United, accessed June 22, 2020, https://www.bornleadersunited.com/humanize-my-hoodie.

10. "Humanize My Hoodie," Born Leaders United, accessed June 22, 2020, https://www.bornleadersunited.com/humanize-my-hoodie.

11. S. Banerji, "Study: Darker-Skinned Black Job Applicants Hit More Obstacles," Diverse Issues in Higher Education, August 31, 2006, https://diverseeducation.com/article/6306/.

12. A. Ben-Zeev et al., "When an 'Educated' Black Man Becomes Lighter in the Mind's Eye: Evidence for a Skin Tone Memory Bias," *SAGE Open* 4, no. 1 (January 2014), https://doi.org/10.1177/2158244013516770.

13. S. Devaraj, N. R. Quigley, and P. C. Patel, "The Effects of Skin Tone, Height, and Gender on Earnings," *PLoS ONE* 13, no. 1 (2018): e0190640, https://doi.org/10.1371/journal.pone.0190640.

14. D. J. Travis and J. Thorpe-Moscon, *Day-to-Day Experiences of Emotional Tax among Women and Men of Color in the Workplace* (Catalyst, February 15, 2018), https://www.catalyst.org/research/day-to-day-experiences-of-emotional-tax-among-women-and-men-of-color-in-the-workplace/.

15. "About Us," Intercultural Development Inventory, accessed June 22, 2020, https://idiinventory.com/about-us/.

16. NewsOne staff, "83 Black Men and Boys Killed by Police," NewsOne, June 2, 2020, https://newsone.com/playlist/black-men-boy-who-were-killed-by-police/item/1.

17. S. Sinyangwe, "Police Killed 1,099 People in 2019," Mapping Police Violence, accessed April 28, 2020, https://mappingpoliceviolence.org/.

18. A. J. Willingham, "Researchers Studied Nearly 100 Million Traffic Stops and Found Black Motorists Are More Likely to Be Pulled Over," CNN, March 21, 2019, https://www.cnn.com/2019/03/21/us/police-stops-race-stanford-study-trnd/index.html.

19. "Race and the Drug War," Drug Policy Alliance, accessed June 8, 2020, https://www.drugpolicy.org/issues/race-and-drug-war.

20. "Report to the United Nations on Racial Disparities in the U.S. Criminal Justice System," Sentencing Project, April 19, 2018, https://www.sentencingproject.org/publications/un-report-on-racial-disparities/.

21. "Black Marriage in America," Black Demographics, accessed June 22, 2020, https://blackdemographics.com/households/marriage-in-black-america/.

22. R. Chetty et al., "Race and Economic Opportunity in the United States: An Intergenerational Perspective," March 2018, http://www.equality-of-opportunity.org/assets/documents/race_paper.pdf.

23. G. Lopez, "Report: Black Men Get Longer Sentences for the Same Federal Crime as White Men," Vox, November 17, 2017, https://www.vox.com/identities/2017/11/17/16668770/us-sentencing-commission-race-booker.

24. K. L. Gilbert et al., "Visible and Invisible Trends in Black Men's Health: Pitfalls and Promises for Addressing Racial, Ethnic, and Gender Inequities in Health," *Annual Review of Public Health* 37 (2016): 295–311, https://doi.org/10.1146/annurev-publhealth-032315-021556.

25. N. Torres, "Research: Having a Black Doctor Led Black Men to Receive More-Effective Care," *Harvard Business Review*, August 10, 2018, https://hbr.org/2018/08/research-having-a-black-doctor-led-black-men-to-receive-more-effective-care.

26. H. Neighbors, "'Manning Up' Can Often Bring Men Down," Association of American Medical Colleges, July 14, 2019, https://www.aamc.org/news-insights/manning-can-often-bring-men-down.

27. "Our History," Confess Project, accessed June 25, 2020, https://www.theconfessproject.com/our-vision-1.

28. Men Thrive homepage, accessed June 25, 2020, https://www.menthrive.com/.

29. R. Ellison, *Invisible Man* (New York: Vintage International, 1995), 572.

30. J. A. Degruy, *Post Traumatic Slave Syndrome: America's Legacy of Enduring Injury and Healing* (n.p.: Joy Degruy Publications, 2005).

31. K. Crenshaw, "Beyond Racism and Misogyny: Black Feminism and 2 Live Crew," *Boston Review*, accessed April 28, 2020, http://bostonreview.net/archives/BR16.6/crenshaw.html.

32. F. Jones, "Why Black Women Struggle More with Domestic Violence," *Time*, September 10, 2014, https://time.com/3313343/ray-rice-black-women-domestic-violence/.

33. "Divorce Statistics: Over 115 Studies, Facts and Rates for 2018," Wilkinson & Finkbeiner, accessed June 22, 2020, https://www.wf-lawyers.com/divorce-statistics-and-facts/.

34. M. Smiley, "Collective Responsibility," in *The Stanford Encyclopedia of Philosophy* (Summer 2017 ed.), ed. Edward N. Zalta, https://plato.stanford.edu/entries/collective-responsibility/.

Chapter Eight

1. "K-12 Disparity Facts and Statistics," United Negro College Fund, accessed April 30, 2020, https://uncf.org/pages/k-12-disparity-facts-and-stats.

2. "Joint 'Dear Colleague' Letter," Office of Civil Rights, January 8, 2014, https://www2.ed.gov/about/offices/list/ocr/letters/colleague-201401-title-vi.html.

3. "What's the Racial Breakdown of America's Public School Teachers?," The 74, August 4, 2018, https://www.the74million.org/article/whats-the-racial-breakdown-of-americas-public-school-teachers/.

4. K. Weir, "Inequality at School," *Monitor on Psychology* 47, no. 10 (2016): 42, https://www.apa.org/monitor/2016/11/cover-inequality-school.

5. K. Legette, "School Tracking and Youth Self-Perceptions: Implications for Academic and Racial Identity," *Child Development* 89, no. 4 (2018): 1311–1327.

6. "Efficacy—a Singular Mission: Move All Children to Rigorous Standards of Academic Proficiency," Efficacy Institute, accessed June 22, 2020, https://www.efficacy.org/.

7. S. Tatum, "As Learning Moves Online, Coronavirus Highlights a Growing Digital Divide," ABC News, April 25, 2020, https://abcnews.go.com/Politics/learning-moves-online-coronavirus-highlights-growing-digital-divide/story?id=70238572.

8. "The Significance of the 'Doll Test,'" Legal Defense and Educational Fund, accessed October 20, 2019, https://www.naacpldf.org/ldf-celebrates-60th-anniversary-brown-v-board-education/significance-doll-test/.

9. E. N. Winkler, "Children Are Not Colorblind: How Young Children Learn Race," *PACE* 3, no. 3 (2009): 1–8, https://inclusions.org/wp-content/uploads/2017/11/Children-are-Not-Colorblind.pdf.

10. "Children in Poverty by Race and Ethnicity in the United States," Kids Count Data Center, last updated September 2019, https://datacenter.kidscount.org/data/tables/44-children-in-poverty-by-race-and-ethnicity#detailed/1/any/false/37,871,870,573,869,36,868,867,133,38/10,11,9,12,1,185,13/324,323.

11. "Children in Single-Parent Families by Race in the United States," Kids Count Data Center, last updated January 2020, https://datacenter.kidscount.org/data/tables/107-children-in-single-parent-families-by-race#detailed/1/any/false/37,871,870,573,869,36,868,867,133,38/10,11,9,12,1,185,13/432,431.

12. P. A. Goff et al., "The Essence of Innocence: Consequences of Dehumanizing Black Children," *Journal of Personality and Social Psychology* 106, no. 4 (2014): 526–545, https://doi.org/10.1037/a0035663.

13. R. Epstein, J. J. Blake, and T. Gonzalez, *Girlhood Interrupted: The Erasure of Black Girls' Childhood* (Center on Poverty and Inequality, accessed April 30, 2020), https://www.law.georgetown.edu/poverty-inequality-center/wp-content/uploads/sites/14/2017/08/girlhood-interrupted.pdf.

14. T. Coates, *Between the World and Me* (New York: Spiegel and Grau, 2015).

15. "Having 'the Talk': Expert Guidance on Preparing Kids for Police Interactions," NPR, August 27, 2029, https://www.npr.org/local/309/2019/08/27/754459083/having-the-talk-expert-guidance-on-preparing-kids-for-police-interactions.

16. G. Johnson, "Toxic Stress and Children's Outcomes and the State of Research on In-School Sources of Trauma," Opportunity Institute, May 3, 2019, https://theopportunityinstitute.org/blog/toxic-stress-and-childrens-outcomes-and-the-state-of-research-on-in-school-sources-of-trauma.

17. P. Parker, "Many Countries Pay Parents for Having Kids in an Effort to Reduce Poverty," State of Opportunity, May 31, 2016, https://stateofopportunity.michiganradio.org/post/many-countries-pay-parents-having-kids-effort-reduce-poverty.

18. J. Tehrani, "Three Companies That Are Helping To Combat Food Deserts," December 21, 2018, https://buzzbinpadillaco.com/three-companies-helping-combat-food-deserts/.

Chapter Nine

1. Chris Crass homepage, accessed June 23, 2020, http://www.chriscrass.org/.

2. C. Crass, *Towards the "Other America": Anti-racist Resources for White People Taking Action for Black Lives Matter* (Saint Louis, MO: Chalice, 2016).

3. Showing Up for Racial Justice homepage, accessed June 24, 2020, https://www.showingupforracialjustice.org/.

4. A. Gordon-Reed, "America's Original Sin: Slavery and the Legacy of White Supremacy," *Foreign Affairs*, January/February 2018, http://cf.linnbenton.edu/artcom/social_science/clarkd/upload/America's%20Original%20Sin.pdf.

5. R. Ray and A. M. Perry, "Why We Need Reparations for Black Americans," Brookings, April 15, 2020, https://www.brookings.edu/policy2020/bigideas/why-we-need-reparations-for-black-americans/.

6. D. Yaffe, "Seminary Pledges to Set Aside $27.6 Million as Reparations for Its Ties to Slavery," *Princeton Alumni Weekly*, November 13, 2019, https://paw.princeton.edu/article/seminary-pledges-set-aside-276-million-reparations-its-ties-slavery.

7. Your Black World, "Shocking List of 10 Companies that Profited from the Slave Trade," https://www.racism.org/index.php/articles/law-and-justice/citizenship-rights/117-slavery-to-reparations/reparations/1697-reparations1001.

8. C. Turner et al., "Why America's Schools Have a Money Problem," NPR, April 18, 2016, https://www.npr.org/2016/04/18/474256366/why-americas-schools-have-a-money-problem#:~:text=In%20the%20U.S.%2C%20school%20fund.

9. I. X. Kendi, *How to Be an Antiracist* (New York: Random House, 2019).

10. "Being Antiracist," National Museum of African American History and Culture, Smithsonian, accessed June 22, 2020, https://nmaahc.si.edu/learn/talking-about-race/topics/being-antiracist.

11. H. Ziady, "Why Ben & Jerry's Statement on White Supremacy Is So Extraordinary," CNN, June 5, 2020, https://www.cnn.com/2020/06/03/business/ben—jerrys-george-floyd/index.html.

12. A. Lamont, "Guide to Allyship," accessed June 22, 2020, https://guidetoallyship.com/.

ACKNOWLEDGMENTS

I am blessed with a circle of family, friends, mentors, and colleagues who are always there to provide love, support, and encouragement—too many to name them all here, but I would like to acknowledge some. First, my adult children and their spouses: Dr. Joseph Winters (son), Dr. Kamilah Legette (daughter-in-law), Mareisha Reese (daughter), and Byron Reese (son-in-law). Joseph is a tenured associate professor of religion at Duke University. He specializes in critical race theory, and besides being a loving son, he was a great thought partner in developing the concepts for this book. Kamilah is a research associate at the University of North Carolina at Chapel Hill. She studies the impact of racial bias in educational environments and was also a helpful thought partner. I reference some of her research in the book. Mareisha serves as chief operating officer for The Winters Group and is a daily inspiration, constantly helping me to think more clearly and practically about my ideas. Mareisha's husband, Byron, is supportive and loving and a wonderful champion of The Winters Group. He is present at all of our events, helping behind the scenes to ensure our success.

I acknowledge my late partner, Kenneth Newby, who passed away on December 8, 2019. He was always there, loving me and supporting my work. My extended family includes his children,

Kenton and Cicily Newby, and their children, Olivia and Savannah. We share a special bond of love that I will always cherish. Family is everything, and while I cannot name everyone, I am grateful for the support of my brother, sisters-in-law, nieces, nephews, and cousins.

Every amazing member of The Winters Group team has participated in some way in the production of this book. They reviewed each chapter and provided invaluable feedback. They are the following:

Kevin Carter, principal strategist
Megan Ellinghausen, marketing and branding associate
Brittany J. Harris, vice president, learning and innovation
Travis Jones, principal strategist
Leigh Morrison, manager, learning and innovation
Krystle Nicholas, project and financial analyst
Chevara Orrin, principal strategist
Katelyn Peterson, public relations and events coordinator
Mareisha Reese, chief operating officer
Keley Smith Miller, operations manager
Thamara Subramanian, manager, learning and innovation
Valda Valbrun, principal strategist
Bahiyyah Walker, principal strategist

I give a special shout-out to Katelyn Peterson, who was most intimately involved as research assistant and editor. As with my first Berrett-Koehler book, Steve Piersanti and many others at BK provided me with invaluable insights and kept pushing me (in caring ways) to be more succinct. I acknowledge the support of my special circle of friends, including Marcia Fugate, Tina DaCosta, Gail Livingston, Odaris Jordan, Mildred Campbell,

Carmen Brown, Charlotte Downing, Peggy Harvey Lee, Carol Champ, Irene Bradley, Mary Patton, Delores Geter, Marie Rivers, Brenda Caine, and Gabrielle Webster.

Finally, I acknowledge all the diversity and inclusion practitioners who work tirelessly every day in pursuit of justice for all, especially the "Diversity Divas," with whom I daily share the joys, successes, frustrations, and disappointments that come with this work.

INDEX

Note: Page numbers followed by *f* indicate a figure on the corresponding page.

ABOUT THE AUTHOR

Mary-Frances Winters came of age during the civil rights movement of the 1960s. Starting with her days as editor of her high school newspaper, Winters realized that diversity, equity, and inclusion work is her "passion and calling." Founding The Winters Group was the next step in fulfilling what she believes is her true purpose on this earth—breaking down barriers and building bridges across differences. As CEO of The Winters Group for the past thirty-six years, Winters has been able to magnify the impact of her thought-provoking message and has gained extensive experience in working with senior leadership teams to drive organizational change.

Among her many awards and distinctions, Winters received the Winds of Change Award, conferred by the University of St. Thomas at the Forum on Workplace Inclusion, for her efforts to change lives, organizations, and communities. She has served as a torchbearer for the Olympics and has been recognized as an ATHENA Leadership Award winner from the Chamber of

Commerce for her professional excellence and for actively assisting women in their attainment of professional excellence. Winters received the Hutchinson Medal from her alma mater, the University of Rochester, in recognition of outstanding achievement and notable service to the community, state, or nation. She has also been recognized as a diversity pioneer by *Profiles in Diversity Journal* and named by *Forbes* as one of the top 10 trailblazers in diversity and inclusion.

Winters is a life member of the Board of Trustees of the University of Rochester and has served on the boards of the Chamber of Commerce, United Way, and the National Board of Girl Scouts of the USA. She is the author of five other books: *Inclusive Conversations: Fostering Equity, Empathy, and Belonging across Differences*; *We Can't Talk about That at Work! How to Talk about Race, Religion, Politics, and Other Polarizing Topics*; *Only Wet Babies Like Change: Workplace Wisdom for Baby Boomers*; *Inclusion Starts with "I"*; and *CEOs Who Get It: Diversity Leadership from the Heart and Soul*. She also wrote a chapter for the book *Diversity at Work: The Practice of Inclusion* and numerous articles.

Winters has influenced hundreds of organizations and thousands of individuals who often describe her as thoughtful, credible, results oriented, and innovative. She is known as a provocateur, especially in sharing the importance of Bold, Inclusive Conversations, an initiative that was developed to encourage organizations to create brave spaces and have dialogues about difficult workplace topics such as race, religion, and politics.

ABOUT THE WINTERS GROUP, INC.

The Winters Group, Inc., is a certified minority- and women-owned global diversity and inclusion consulting firm headquartered in Charlotte, North Carolina. For more than three decades, The Winters Group has supported leaders and organizations, large and small, with developing transformative, sustainable solutions for equity and inclusion. The Winters Group has partnered with hundreds of organizations to develop, execute, and measure strategies that foster inclusion and lead to breakthrough results.

The Winters Group envisions a world that values, respects, and leverages our similarities and differences. Some of The Winters Group's unique offerings include the following:

- diversity, equity, and inclusion strategy development
- cultural audits (surveys, focus groups, and interviews)
- learning and education
- change management
- executive coaching
- keynote speaking and conference facilitation
- Engaging in Bold, Inclusive Conversations certification
- Fostering Cultural Competence certification
- Understanding Identity and Building Bridges

- Mapping the Intersection of Inclusion and Social Justice
- Radical Inclusion certification
- Racial Justice Institute
- Em*POWER*ment Institute
- Cracking the Code of Unconscious Bias
- Diversity, Equity, and Inclusion Facilitator Institute certification

Since its inception in 2018, The Winters Group corporate social responsibility arm, Live Inclusively Actualized, has given $150,000 in grants to 501(c)(3) organizations dedicated to breaking down systemic barriers for marginalized women and youths.

5. How do we ensure inclusion and not tokenism of Black members on your team?
6. To what extent is our language and behavior antiracist versus nonracist?
7. To what extent do we intentionally or unintentionally look for "fit" on our team?
8. Has the team environment we have cultivated indirectly encouraged team members to downplay distinguishing factors of their identity to fit in?
9. What explicit efforts do we/can we take to educate ourselves about race and racism?
10. What do microagressions sound like on your team?
11. What team norms can you create to foster ongoing education to ensure that your culture is inclusive?

Organization

1. In what ways does your organization have a white supremacist culture?
2. To what extent have you examined your policies and practices for unintended racism (e.g., hiring barriers, pay inequities, outmoded job requirements)? Do you lump all diversity dimensions together, or do you examine each dimension?
3. Have you surveyed employees to gauge their perceptions about diversity and inclusion in your organization?
4. In what ways is the organization complicit in perpetuating racism (silence, distancing, denying, placating)?
5. Does your representation at all levels mirror the communities that you serve? Are Black people clustered at the lower levels and underrepresented in leadership? Why?
6. How do your diversity, equity, and inclusion programs address systemic racism?
7. What is the history of your organization related to racist practices (e.g., was it involved in slavery, redlining, Jim Crow, employment discrimination)? If there is a history, what restorative measures have you taken?
8. How is the organizational leadership held accountable for fostering antiracism?
9. Is the retention of Black employees a concern? Do you know why Black employees leave? Are the reasons different than for white employees?
10. To what extent are the voices of historically marginalized people an integral part of decision making?

BK

Berrett-Koehler Discussion Guide

Black Fatigue

How Racism Erodes the Mind, Body, and Spirit

By Mary-Frances Winters

I hope that reading *Black Fatigue* provided some new insights for you about the causes and impacts of racism and what we need to do to dismantle ingrained white supremacist ideology. It may have also raised some new questions that would be beneficial to explore with your professional and/or personal circles.

The discussion prompts are meant to be considered at the **individual**, **team**, and **organizational** levels.

Individual

1. Who am I in the context of a racialized society? To what extent is race a core aspect of my identity? If it is not core, why not?
2. How does my race influence how I see myself and how others see me?
3. What does it mean to be white?
4. What does it mean to be Black or another nonwhite identity?
5. How do my intersecting identities (e.g., race, gender, age, sexual orientation) influence how I see myself and how others see me?
6. What narratives or cultural scripts have I learned about race?
7. What characteristics associated with whiteness have I internalized as the norm?
8. How am I complicit in perpetuating racist systems (e.g., silence, denial, defense)?
9. How can I use my power in my home, in my school, in my place of worship, with friends, with work associates, and in other spheres of influence to foster antiracism?
10. What can I personally do to mitigate Black fatigue (my own or others')?

Team

1. To what extent is race the "elephant in the room" on your team?
2. To what extent is the team comfortable talking about race?
3. What is the source of your discomfort?
4. If you are the leader, how would you characterize your relationship with your Black employees? Do you conduct regular listening sessions? Do Black employees feel safe speaking up? Do you know the sources of Black fatigue among your team?

Also by Mary-Frances Winters

We Can't Talk about That at Work!

How to Talk about Race, Religion, Politics, and Other Polarizing Topics

Conversations about taboo topics happen at work every day. And if they aren't handled effectively, they can become polarizing and divisive, impacting productivity, engagement, retention, and employees' sense of safety in the workplace. In this concise and powerful book, Mary-Frances Winters shows how to deal with sensitive subjects in a way that brings people together instead of driving them apart. She helps you become aware of the role culture plays in shaping people's perceptions, habits, and communication styles and gives detailed guidance for structuring conversations about those things we're not supposed to talk about.

Paperback, ISBN 978-1-5230-9426-4
PDF ebook, ISBN 978-1-5230-9427-1
ePub ebook ISBN 978-1-5230-9428-8
Digital audio, ISBN 978-1-5230-9425-7

Berrett–Koehler Publishers, Inc.
www.bkconnection.com

800.929.2929

Berrett–Koehler Publishers

Berrett-Koehler is an independent publisher dedicated to an ambitious mission: *Connecting people and ideas to create a world that works for all.*

Our publications span many formats, including print, digital, audio, and video. We also offer online resources, training, and gatherings. And we will continue expanding our products and services to advance our mission.

We believe that the solutions to the world's problems will come from all of us, working at all levels: in our society, in our organizations, and in our own lives. Our publications and resources offer pathways to creating a more just, equitable, and sustainable society. They help people make their organizations more humane, democratic, diverse, and effective (and we don't think there's any contradiction there). And they guide people in creating positive change in their own lives and aligning their personal practices with their aspirations for a better world.

And we strive to practice what we preach through what we call "The BK Way." At the core of this approach is *stewardship,* a deep sense of responsibility to administer the company for the benefit of all of our stakeholder groups, including authors, customers, employees, investors, service providers, sales partners, and the communities and environment around us. Everything we do is built around stewardship and our other core values of *quality, partnership, inclusion,* and *sustainability.*

This is why Berrett-Koehler is the first book publishing company to be both a B Corporation (a rigorous certification) and a benefit corporation (a for-profit legal status), which together require us to adhere to the highest standards for corporate, social, and environmental performance. And it is why we have instituted many pioneering practices (which you can learn about at www.bkconnection.com), including the Berrett-Koehler Constitution, the Bill of Rights and Responsibilities for BK Authors, and our unique Author Days.

We are grateful to our readers, authors, and other friends who are supporting our mission. We ask you to share with us examples of how BK publications and resources are making a difference in your lives, organizations, and communities at www.bkconnection.com/impact.

Dear reader,

Thank you for picking up this book and welcome to the worldwide BK community! You're joining a special group of people who have come together to create positive change in their lives, organizations, and communities.

What's BK all about?

Our mission is to connect people and ideas to create a world that works for all.

Why? Our communities, organizations, and lives get bogged down by old paradigms of self-interest, exclusion, hierarchy, and privilege. But we believe that can change. That's why we seek the leading experts on these challenges—and share their actionable ideas with you.

A welcome gift

To help you get started, we'd like to offer you a **free copy** of one of our bestselling ebooks:

www.bkconnection.com/welcome

When you claim your **free ebook**, you'll also be subscribed to our blog.

Our freshest insights

Access the best new tools and ideas for leaders at all levels on our blog at ideas.bkconnection.com.

Sincerely,

Your friends at Berrett-Koehler